Empowered by the Spirit to Win and Disciple New Believers

SOUL WINNER

The dear writer of *Soulwinner* taught me all the things that she has written in this book. She spent long hours and used much patience to teach me, love me, and explain how important it is to be faithful to the things of God. Because of all her work, prayers, and listening to the Lord, I can say eleven years later that I am teaching and getting the privilege to win people to the Lord!

MELANIE PETERMAN

From the first time that I met Dawn Kurtz, it was evident that Jesus was living within her. The Holy Spirit within her was showing. When she informed me of her desire to write a book on soulwinning and gave me its overview, I immediately encouraged her to do so. The result is outstanding.

The fast moving, crisp style and her insight, along with her personal experiences, keep the reader attentive while absorbing the Christ-centered contents.

You will find the book thought provoking and propelling, inspirational and insightful. It is full of sound soulwinning principles, which are practical and easy to implement. The examples from Bible times and the present day make the book's contents applicable in today's world.

From preparing your own heart to reaching out to the lost, from greeting visitors at the church to developing new believers into consistent Christians and fruitful soulwinners, this book is a godsend and will meet one of the greatest needs within the apostolic church.

Indeed the Holy Spirit is already at work within you, and the contents of this book will help you set Him free to bring forth fruit in your life.

PASTOR G. A. TRACY
New Life Pentecostal Church, Bridgeton, MO

Written with love for the lost and a heartfelt desire to see young Christians established in the faith, *Soulwinner* is a great encourager to all who love lost humanity. Dawn Kurtz declares the priority of the church: evangelism. Soulwinning does not end at the baptistery and the altar: in this book, we are summoned to nourish and to serve those newly won to the Lord. You will find this study inspiring and instructive as the author's zeal is transmitted through her message. If we are designated as being wise for winning souls, then this is an accelerated lesson to bring us biblical wisdom.

PASTOR RODNEY V. PAMER
Apostolic Church of Barberton, OH

Empowered by the Spirit to Win and Disciple
New Believers

SOUL WINNER

DAWN M. KURTZ

Soulwinner:
Empowered by the Spirit to Win and Disciple New Believers

by Dawn M. Kurtz

Hazelwood, MO 63042-2299

Cover Design by Paul Povolni

All Scripture quotations in this book are from the King James Version of the Bible unless otherwise identified.

Printed in United States of America

Printed by

WORD AFLAME® PRESS
8855 DUNN ROAD
HAZELWOOD, MO 63042-2299

Library of Congress Cataloging-in-Publication Data

Kurtz, Dawn M.
Soulwinner / Dawn M. Kurtz.
p. cm.
ISBN 1-56722-586-1
1. Evangelistic work. I. Title.

BV3770.K88 2002
269'.2—dc21 2002069164

Dedication

Soulwinner is dedicated to King Jesus, who is the ultimate soulwinner, and to His children who hunger to win souls for the kingdom of God.

And also to my husband, Bob, who shares the hope of salvation for our children, their children, and their children's children. "For what is our hope, or joy, or crown of rejoicing? Are not even ye in the presence of our Lord Jesus Christ at his coming? For ye are our glory and joy" (I Thessalonians 2:19-20).

And finally, to my dear friend Melanie, whose victories in life reflect the Savior's saving grace.

Contents

PREFACE

"And, behold, I send the promise of my Father upon you: but tarry ye in the city of Jerusalem, until ye be *endued with power* from on high" (Luke 24:49, emphasis mine).

"But ye shall receive power, after that the Holy Ghost is come upon you: and ye *shall be witnesses* unto me both in Jerusalem, and in all Judaea, and in Samaria, and unto the uttermost part of the earth" (Acts 1:8, emphasis mine).

Prior to His ascension, the resurrected Jesus commanded His followers to go to Jerusalem and wait for a supernatural power. He explained that this power would be from the Holy Spirit and that it would empower them to tell others about the gospel. After the apostles went back to Jerusalem, they and many other disciples, about 120 persons, tarried in an upper room, worshiping and praising God, while waiting for the fulfillment of Jesus' promise. Suddenly, a wind began to blow violently within the room. Can you imagine their surprise as flames of fire appeared above each of their heads and something began to bubble up from deep within them, causing them to burst forth in an unknown language? For the first time in the history of mankind, God had filled man with His Spirit.

The noise from the upper room was so great that it caught the attention of those outside on the streets. The astonished crowd could hear shouts of praise in many of the different languages of the regions surrounding Jerusalem. Perhaps they also saw the disciples dancing wildly and flailing their arms toward heaven. We do not know exactly how the disciples were acting, but it caused some in the crowd to shout, "They are drunk," while others wondered and questioned how these simple Galileans could speak so many languages.

Hearing the crowd's comments, Peter stood and lifted his voice above the din and began to explain the phenomenon that was taking place. A hush came over the crowd as Peter revealed to them that a prophecy in the Book of Joel regarding the end times was beginning to be fulfilled: "Ye men of Judaea, and all *ye* that dwell at Jerusalem, be this known unto you, and hearken to my words: For these are not drunken, as ye suppose, seeing it is *but* the third hour of the day. But this is that which was spoken by the prophet Joel; And it shall come to pass in the last days, saith God, *I will pour out of my Spirit upon all flesh:* and your sons and your daughters shall prophesy, and your young men shall see visions, and your old men shall dream dreams: And on my servants and on my handmaidens I will pour out in those days of my Spirit; and *they shall prophesy"* (Acts 2:14-18, emphasis mine).

Since this spectacular event when God first came to

abide within man, the Holy Spirit continues to partner Himself with born-again men and women, empowering them to prophesy or to teach the gospel. Once we are born again, a phenomenal change occurs in us—we become a new creation in Christ (II Corinthians 5:17)! But the change is not just for us personally; the Holy Spirit endows us with supernatural power to win others for Him (Acts 1:8).

On the Day of Pentecost, God ignited the flames of revival and produced the first soulwinners empowered by His Spirit. Men such as Peter, John, and Andrew had been fishermen. Their born-again experience converted them from common fishermen to "fishers of men" (Matthew 4:19). Mary and the other women would never again be mere housewives. They would open their homes for worship and prayer meetings. In every generation since the birth of the church, the Spirit of God continues to change people's lives. Not only does the Spirit change us, He empowers us to share the gospel with others and to help establish new believers in the church. As we grow in grace, the Spirit also dampens cravings to build kingdoms of fame and fortune, as He rains down on us a desire to enlarge the kingdom of God.

I begin this book with my testimony of how God called me into His kingdom and filled me with His Spirit, which forever changed the course of my life. Today, just as on the day when I was born again of His Spirit, I still feel chosen by God; hence the title of part one: *Chosen to Serve.* In this section, I reveal how, at a young age, God began to work on my heart. Whether it happened yesterday or many years ago, it is my sincere hope that you will be stirred to recall the day when God filled you with His Spirit and changed the purpose of your life. As God's ambassadors to this world, we must keep alive the enthusiasm that we felt at the moment when God filled us with His Spirit. It is this enthusiasm that will cause us to choose to lead others to God. When we choose to serve God, we are obeying the great commission.

In part two, *Choosing to Serve,* I discuss the command to spread the gospel, techniques used in soulwinning, and practical advice in teaching home Bible studies.

Finally, in part three, *Serving,* I share aspects of my relationship with a new convert, as I helped her to grow into maturity in Christ. Like our natural children, some spiritually born babies require more attention than others. This heartwarming account of a one-on-one relationship illustrates the merits of discipleship that often involve nurturing or travailing until the new baby in Christ reaches a place of maturity to stand on his or her own two feet.

There are pastors, missionaries, evangelists, and persons from the Bible, such as Paul, who have won thousands to the kingdom of God. I have not done that. But over the years, I have had many experiences in soulwinning that I want to share with readers who desire to win someone to God. It is my earnest prayer that you may lose any fear that you may have about teaching a home Bible study or about just talking to someone about our Savior. I do not have all the answers to soulwinning, but I do know that God works through *willing* vessels. What I have done and experienced in soulwinning, you can do and more if you will trust God to use you.

When we win a soul for Christ, He receives all the glory—we have nothing to boast about. We must remember that it is the Holy Spirit who works *within us* to reach the lost. Our gender, age, race or nationality, or talents do not matter—what matters is that God loves all people and desires to partner Himself with us to spread His precious gospel. We can lead others to Christ if we will allow God's Holy Spirit to work through us.

God's Spirit plus a willing vessel
equals a soulwinner!

Part One

CHOSEN TO SERVE

*"Ye have not chosen me,
but I have chosen you, and ordained you,
that ye should go and bring forth fruit"
(John 15:16).*

Chosen

Late September, with frost's first execution,
Sends autumn leaves spiraling in scattered profusion—
Leaves neon bright, green, orange, and yellow,
Not yet crisp, but soft and mellow.
One stood out from all the others, so perfect in its design,
A tiny, sugar maple leaf no bigger than a dime.
Salvaged from that compost pile and carefully tucked away
Between the pages of a Bible carried that momentous day.
So sweetly cries the love of Jesus each time the leaf I view,
"Dear child, out of all this world, I have chosen you."

DMK

CHAPTER ONE

My Spiritual Birth

The poem "Chosen" is based on an event that happened in my life. One day as I was walking in the fields behind my church, I looked down and saw a tiny, sugar maple leaf lying amidst countless leaves. As I bent over and picked it up, the thought occurred to me that I was like that tiny leaf. I understand that God is not a respecter of persons, but at that moment, I felt so blessed that God had found me and had chosen me from among the billions of people across all time and generations. I quickly tucked the little leaf between the pages of my Bible. Every time I open to the first page of Proverbs, I see the leaf that I had chosen from that pile of innumerable leaves and am reminded that from out of billions of people, Jesus chose me!

Jesus wrought a great change in my life the day He

filled me with the Holy Spirit. Since my conversion, all that I am and everything that I hope to be is in Jesus. He is my life today and hope for eternity. Before I came to the Lord, my life was meaningless. It was, in fact, without form and void as the earth is described in Genesis 1:2. I did not know where I was going in life; but fortunately, I did know to Whom I belonged. I hungered to know my Creator. And unlike Job, I did know where to find Him. As a child, I was taken to church on occasion, but not always where true salvation was taught. I became God-conscious at a very young age because my mother talked to me about God and taught me to pray before bedtime and meals.

Although my natural birth was one of the most exciting events in my mother's life, to the world, I was just another number to tabulate in the census. However, my spiritual birth was a different story. The news of my baptism into the family of God caused the heavenly host to rejoice! I was the center of attraction in my own special miracle. Great rejoicing took place in my heart and in heaven as my name was etched into the Lamb's Book of Life. My soul discovered the ultimate definition of joy—and the angels gave a party! I know it is hard to imagine that we are worth that much excitement in heaven, but note what Jesus said about our new birth: "I say unto you, that likewise joy shall be in heaven over one sinner that repenteth, more than over ninety and nine just persons, which need no repentance" (Luke 15:7).

The steps leading to the exciting event of my salvation might have begun the day my mother dedicated me to the Lord in a nearby Wesleyan Methodist church. Mother didn't know too much about the Word of God at that time, but she did have a desire for her children to be saved. She acted on all she knew. (Later, God would lead us both into the full gospel truth.)

God's Word began to open up to me on Christmas Day in 1964 when I received my first white, zippered Bible. I was nine years old at the time. In awe, I began to read about Jesus who died on the cross for me. I read, "For God so loved the world, that he gave his only begotten Son, that whosoever believeth in him should not perish, but have everlasting life" (John 3:16). Somehow, I knew that the part about "whosoever" was referring to me. No one taught me how to read my Bible, but I learned to cherish the words within its gold-edged pages.

On several occasions during that same time period, my grandparents took me to their Pentecostal church. I loved Sunday school, and I loved the music. Worship seemed as natural as breathing to me.

Those early experiences in an apostolic church planted seeds of truth that lay dormant until six years later at age fifteen. One day, in the middle of high school band class, I began to cry uncontrollably from deep within. I had no idea at that time that my soul was thirsting for living water. The tears flowed as my teacher sent me to the school principal. He asked if I was having problems with any of my teachers. Frantically, I searched my brain for a response that might explain my obvious emotional distress. Instantly, my Spanish teacher came to mind. I told the school principal about this man, who seemed half-crazy from his experience as a prisoner of war during the Korean War. Old Mr. Kiba spent most of our class hour telling us about the horrible torture he endured as a prisoner of war and about the ungratefulness of American youth. Horrid as his stories were, I didn't really believe in my heart that I was crying over Mr. Kiba's stories. Although I didn't mention it to the principal, my mind was reflecting on the general condition of the kids in my graduating class. Our class motto was "Crime, Sex, and LSD, we're the Class of '73." Drugs, alcohol, and hard rock music—where did I fit into all this? I didn't. I knew that I was different. On the day the dam broke, my rose-colored glasses fell off in that flood of tears. I cried for the corrupt decadence of my world and, as I would discover later, for the apparent hopeless condition of my soul.

After school, I threw myself on my bed and continued to cry. Mother came to my room and asked me what was wrong. I don't remember what I babbled, but in her motherly wisdom, she simply said, "I think you need God." Mom took me to an apostolic church that Sunday, and I loved it. We returned for the evening service. It was then that I first saw the importance of the blood of Jesus and was compelled to plunge under its crimson flow. I quickly walked to the altar while the church sang, "Come Home, Come Home, It's Supper Time." I came to Jesus just as I was that day, with long, straight, seventies-style hair and a skirt that was too short. Nobody criticized me, and love flowed as the saints prayed. Soon the pastor asked if I would like to be baptized. I eagerly said, "Yes!" It was so wonderful. I went down into very cold baptismal waters and came up in a burst of warmth and joy unspeakable.

The night I was baptized, joy stopped my tears, my sins were washed away, and I felt light and free. I still had much to learn about kingdom living, but I knew that I would never fit in with my classmates at school. The line had been drawn in the sand, and I had chosen the Lord's side.

My baptism was truly a glorious experience, but I did not receive the Holy Spirit at that time. In fact, I would not receive the Spirit for over six more years. My intention, of course, had been to always live for the Lord. But I did not have the Spirit or a spiritual mentor to guide my development as a Christian, and as a result, I left the church after only nine months. It always bothered me that I had slipped out of church so easily. But thankfully God guided me back to Him. If God's hand had not been on my life, I would have been lost for eternity! Later when I did return to the apostolic church, I wanted to make sure that no one would ever have a similar experience like I had had, so with the encouragement of the youth pastor, I founded what was called "The Lifeguard Program." This program paired adult saints with young people. As a *lifeguard,* the saint became a friend and mentor to an assigned young person. They prayed for that young person and greeted them at church. Sometimes they bought them gifts on special occasions, such as Christmas or birthdays. While some children have parents in the church, there are others who, like myself as a teenager, have no one to teach them about God's love. The Lifeguard Program proved to be very successful. Even after adulthood, young people continue to include their lifeguard in their lives. Many lifeguards have participated in their young person's wedding, and some have even stood with them at a baby dedication. My theory behind the program was that, when young people have an adult who believes in them, they tend to try to please that adult and therefore stay out of trouble. Also, young people who love their parents or an adult who serves the Lord are more likely to serve God, much like Ruth, who loved Naomi enough to love Naomi's God (Ruth 1:16).

Six years after my baptism, I married a man who was Presbyterian. My husband and I taught Sunday school and were youth leaders at his Presbyterian church. I didn't agree with many of their doctrines, particularly concerning baptism. I even taught my Sunday school class about Acts 2:38 baptism.

Knowing that we should still follow what Peter said, I

spoke to the Presbyterian pastor and his wife about baptism. They simply said, "Different strokes for different folks." Somehow I didn't believe that God's Word was that wishy-washy! I found it quite odd that the Presbyterian pastor allowed me to continue teaching, even though I was firm on teaching Bible rather than tradition.

While still attending the Presbyterian church, I discovered that I was expecting our first child. My maternal instincts took over, and I wanted what was spiritually best for my child. I went to God in prayer. I asked the Lord to lead me into the full truth and to a church where my child would be saved. Meanwhile, my mother invited me to attend a Bible study class being taught at an apostolic church. I don't believe it was a coincidence that this was the same church where I had been baptized six years earlier. I believe God works in all of our lives, leading us step by step into the truth. I attended the classes, and the study more clearly opened my eyes to the truth and caused a longing to attend that church.

Our oldest child was born on a Sunday afternoon. I carried Jason for the entire nine months while attending the Presbyterian church and teaching Sunday school, but after Jason's birth, I never returned there even once. Jason had colic and cried a great deal in his first few weeks, to the point where I was too tired to go anywhere—let alone church. I believe that God was setting in motion the answer to my prayer.

In my heart, I knew that the apostolic church where I had been baptized as a teen and where I had taken the home Bible study course was a church where God's truth was taught and practiced. My husband, however, was not willing to attend an apostolic church. We had visited that church one time several years before with my mother and thought Pentecostal worship strange. However, the power of God and a sincere prayer continued to work. A few weeks after our child's birth, the youth pastor's wife called, and my husband answered the phone. As I spoke with her, she commented on what a nice speaking voice she thought that my husband had, and I relayed the message to him. He smiled and said, "Did she really say that?" I am so glad that God gave us all egos! She had called to invite us to a revival. Bob said that we would go. I kept my composure but was jumping up and down on the inside. God was working it out! I had prayed the prayer that God would lead me into the truth, and now I was willing to step aside and let Him work out the details. To make a long story short, we went to the revival at that church and have never quit going there. As of this writing, in over twenty years after God saved my husband and me, Bob has only missed one Sunday morning service.

God filled me with the Holy Spirit just a few weeks later on November 1, 1977. I don't believe that I will ever experience anything more joyous than the baptism of the Holy Spirit until the day He calls me home. I actually received the Holy Spirit at home rather than at church.

Fortunately, I did not have to tarry week after week at the altar. In fact, I tarried less than a week. I felt a little uncomfortable with people praying out loud around me. While my newborn slept, I went into my bedroom and prayed with all my heart on Monday. While praying again on Tuesday, God filled me with His Spirit. I didn't fully understand what had happened to me, but I claimed the baptism of the Holy Spirit. I even called the pastor and told him about my experience while praying. On the following Sunday during altar call, there was no doubt in anyone's mind that I had indeed received the Holy Spirit. The church received the witness of it! I danced all over that altar area and spoke in tongues for quite some time.

My husband was baptized but seemed to be a bit skeptical about receiving the Holy Spirit and speaking in tongues. I believe he had a certain fear of it. One night at home, while reading our Bibles out loud together, God eliminated Bob's fear. I love this story and tell it to all my Bible study classes. As we were reading, I came to the verse where Jesus said, "I thank thee, O Father, Lord of heaven and earth, because thou hast hid these things from the wise and prudent, and hast revealed them unto babes" (Matthew 11:25). I stopped reading and said to Bob, "Do you realize that Jesus is talking about you and me! We are the babes, and He loved us so much that He has revealed His truth to us!" I got so excited as I was speaking those words that I began to speak in another language! I could not speak English the entire night. Bob stared at me and did what every confused husband should do: he called my mom. I remember him saying, "Here, Mom, talk to her; she is acting crazy!" I took the phone from Mom and spoke in English. When I hung up the phone and tried to talk to Bob, I could not speak English. I began laughing in the Holy Spirit! Bob followed me into the baby's room as I got Jason ready for bed. He wasn't sure if I was sane enough to care for his son. I continued to speak in tongues all night. When it was necessary for me to speak in English, God would allow a word or two. My husband and I lay awake in bed for a very long time. It became so funny. We had great fun with the Holy Spirit until we fell asleep. We would both get quiet for a while, and then Bob would say, "Are you normal yet?" I would start to speak and out would come another language. We laughed and laughed that night. Doesn't God have a wonderful sense of humor? At any rate, Bob lost his fear and soon received the Holy Spirit for himself. I was back to normal in the morning—depending on what you consider normal.

CHAPTER TWO

Not Ashamed of the Gospel

From the womb of repentance, the sinner metamorphoses into a brand-new creature, much like the caterpillar who emerges from its cocoon as a beautiful butterfly. Before its change, the caterpillar is wormlike: ugly, creepy, and crawly. I suppose that without God that is a pretty good description of the lowliness of sinful man! Fortunately, when God's grace changes our lives, we are set free from the bondage of sin, much like the beautiful butterfly whose wings give it freedom to soar above the leaves and branches of the trees. While gravity holds us tightly to the earth for now, someday the Spirit within will defy gravity's hold on God's children, and we will soar toward a place that Jesus has specially prepared for us. "But if the Spirit of him that raised up Jesus from the dead dwell in you, he that raised up Christ from the dead shall also quicken your mortal bodies by his Spirit that dwelleth in you" (Romans 8:11). Soon after salvation takes place, the Holy Spirit stirs newborn children of God to enthusiastically tell everyone who will listen about their conversion. Our testimony is a powerful God-given tool that by design attracts the curiosity of the sinner. Often, after souls are born again, they are invited to share with the congregation how God changed their life. Everyone's story is unique. It is exciting to hear about the mercy of God. Everyone's testimony should be told to the world and shouted from the mountaintops. Unfortunately, not everyone will listen, but there will come a day on the other side of eternity when people from all ages and walks of life will eagerly listen to each and every testimony. Imagine what a glorious time we will have after the trumpet sounds. After that first half-hour of total silence spoken of in the Book of Revelation, we will spend the next few million years worshiping Jesus as the omnipotent King of kings and Redeemer of our souls. And after all that, there will still be eternity for all God's children to tell how Jesus changed their lives.

One thing I love about the state of Missouri is its heritage of storytelling. Missouri is the home of Mark Twain, who was one of the world's greatest storytellers. Storytelling is still a part of Missouri, where Mark Twain's Tom Sawyer and Huck Finn rafted down the Mississippi River. In the fall of every year, a storytelling festival is held on the banks of the Missouri River near the city of Saint

Charles. Professional storytellers captivate their listeners as they spin yarns from the deck of the only remaining original showboat in the world. The listening fun continues as amateurs from the audience are given the microphone to wind a few tales of their own. When you see me in heaven, I will be the one with my arm in the air jumping up and down like an elementary student, "Me next. Pick me next. I want to tell about the miracle of my salvation!" Exuberantly, I will tell how the precious blood of Jesus flowed over centuries of time to miraculously cover all my sins. *Praise the Lord God Almighty!* Although heaven will hold nations and generations of people who have been saved by the blood of Jesus, as far as I am concerned, my own salvation is the greatest of all miracles. I have tried to imagine the excitement in heaven on that day. What a time of jubilee! Why don't you pause for just a moment to reflect on the day God saved your soul. Recall for just a moment your immeasurable joy and how you wanted to tell everyone how God supernaturally set you free from the bondage of sin and forever changed the direction of your life.

New babies in Christ shine with innocence and bubble with excitement after receiving the Holy Spirit. When I received the Holy Spirit, I thought I had found heaven on earth. I had so much joy that when an Avon representative came to my door, I invited her in and told her all about my experience in receiving the Holy Spirit. I spoke unashamedly and with great enthusiasm. I know I was glowing as I told about my supernatural experience. I told her, "Although I knew I had received the Holy Spirit while praying at home, evidently God felt I needed a better experience. I stood there at the altar with my newborn in my arms quietly praying behind my kneeling husband. And then the power hit! My right arm flew up as I held tightly to my baby with my left. Then my left arm shot up as I quickly grabbed the baby with my right arm. The pastor's mother saw what was happening to me and took my baby from my arms. I threw both arms into the air and twirled around that altar area worshiping and praising God in a language I had never learned!" My Avon lady looked quite nervous and quickly disclosed that she was a Jehovah's Witness. I didn't place an order that day, and my Avon lady never returned!

The week after receiving the Holy Spirit, I opened the front door of my house to a man who was dressed exceptionally nice in a black suit with a white dress shirt and tie. I thought he looked like a minister, so I put my hand out and said, "Praise the Lord." He shook my hand and eagerly praised the Lord with me! To my chagrin, I quickly realized that he was a magazine salesman. I am sure my naturally pale face turned crimson. I quickly disappointed my new friend as a "no-sale."

As I have already mentioned, the Avon lady became quite nervous when I told her about my conversion. I didn't really care what the Avon lady or the magazine salesman thought. After all, they were just trying to make a sale, and they remained courteous and non-judgmental, if not somewhat amused by my testimony. However, shortly after my life-changing experience, some things happened that did burst my spiritual bubble.

It didn't take long before the "I am not ashamed of the gospel of Jesus Christ" attitude was challenged. If you will be honest, it probably happened after your conversion also. After my husband and I were born again, our new experience in Christ was not received well by our family or friends. We invited our friends and even family to church. It wasn't very long, however, before we noticed that our friends quit calling and coming to our house. We didn't understand because these were our very best friends. They had been attendants in our wedding. One of them was my husband's best man, and his wife was my maid of honor. We had known them all through school and college. They witnessed our change and apparently wanted no part of our religion. We felt rejected. We began to notice that family members became anxious if we brought up anything about religion or our church. I was beginning to fall below cloud nine. I continued to serve God but became more careful about those I witnessed to and invited to church. I never denied Christ; I just kept Him safely hidden in my weekly worship service.

My enthusiasm was dampened like a smoldering fire. For the first time, I realized that others might not be interested in hearing the gospel. I didn't understand how anyone could reject the Savior who gave His life for us—but they could, I came to find out. Not all people were interested in the miracle of my conversion. My faith waned slightly, and my newfound trust in the Holy Spirit was shaken. Like Adam and Eve, after my eyes were opened, fear replaced my joy. Adam and Eve were afraid for God to discover that they had eaten of the forbidden fruit and were now naked. But why was I afraid? Was I afraid that I would be tortured and thrown in jail like Paul and Silas? No, of course not. Was I afraid that I would be ridiculed? Well, perhaps. But more than likely, I was afraid of rejection. My exuberance had already cost me my friends. Would family excommunicate me as well? Most of us can't handle rejection, and so we quickly squelch the desire to witness. But fortunately, through the Holy Spirit, we have the power within us to overcome this fear.

The Lord knew that we would experience rejection, and He knew how as mortals we would respond; but that did not change the nature of His gospel or His plan that we should spread the gospel. We are not to take rejection personally. Our friends and families are not rejecting us. They may be rejecting God or possibly just the full revelation of His Word. I understand that many of our friends and family who reject our faith do serve God in some capacity or understanding. But they simply refuse to open their hearts to the full revelation of God's Word and, with closed minds, cling to their traditions.

The prophet Samuel also faced rejection. When the people of Israel cried that they wanted a king to rule over them, Samuel took it personally. The Lord comforted Samuel, saying, "They have not rejected thee, but they have rejected me" (I Samuel 8:7). The nation of Israel wanted to be like other nations who were ruled by a king. They no longer trusted the God of all creation to rule them. They wanted a God who was tangible and visible to other nations. Perhaps they thought that it would be easier to live by man's laws instead of God's.

Similarly, people who do not know God in the fullness of His truth want to be in control of their own lives. They don't want to be told what they can and cannot do. They often become nervous in the presence of God's children because God's truth shines so brightly that, like a giant spotlight, it reveals sin and brings conviction to their hearts. This makes people uncomfortable. We must never forget that if it were not for the grace and mercy of God and the light of His truth, we would still be lost in sin. Sometimes we unintentionally make those closest to us feel condemned. If we understand that our family and friends are feeling conviction, it will be easier to love them when we feel rejected by them. Always remember that only love can change the heart of a sinner. As we trust the Spirit within to guide us, we will actually become a part of God's beautiful love triangle: God loves us, we love the sinner, the sinner loves God. God's Spirit will help us lose the fear of rejection as we learn to love all of God's children, no matter how they respond to Christ in us.

After we overcome our fear of rejection, a burden for lost souls again begins to burn from within, like Jeremiah who cried, "But *his word* was in mine heart as a burning fire shut up in my bones, and I was weary with forbearing, and I could not *stay*" (Jeremiah 20:9). We can't help but reach out to the lost, whether poor, depressed, abused, or addicted to alcohol or drugs. As Christ's conduit, if we will allow Him, His love will flow through us to the sinner. His love will lift us above the fear of rejection. The apostle Paul assured us that God did not give us "the spirit of fear; but of power, and of love" (II Timothy 1:7). Recognize that, if God did not give us the spirit of fear, then it is coming from somewhere else. The one who came to steal, kill, and destroy (John 10:10) is the one who fills our hearts with fear. If he can keep us in fear, he knows that we will never share the gospel with anyone.

Hell was not prepared for you and me, but because misery loves company, Satan is determined to take as many of God's children with him to eternal damnation as he can. If we could but catch a vision of sinners falling into the pits of hell, our fear would be replaced with spiritual boldness. Our determination to save a soul would move into high gear. We must understand that, but for the grace of God and someone loving us to Christ, we would be spiraling downward into that chasm of torment. As we grow in Christ and study His Word, the Holy

Spirit fills our mouths with wisdom and the love of a soul becomes greater than our fears. The blessed Spirit of God gives us the necessary power and the boldness to say with determination, "I am not ashamed of the gospel of Christ."

Part Two

CHOOSING TO SERVE

"If any man serve me, let him follow me;
and where I am, there shall also my servant be:
if any man serve me, him will my Father honour"
(John 12:26).

Happy people are those who serve others.
The happiest people are those
who serve others in obedience to God's Word.

CHAPTER THREE

A Servant and a Sower

"Verily, verily, I say unto you, The servant is not greater than his lord; neither he that is sent greater than he that sent him. If ye know these things, happy are ye if ye do them" (John 13:16-17).

Peter couldn't believe what he was seeing. Jesus, his Lord and Master, knelt before one of the disciples to wash his dirty feet. Peter thought, "How could He lower Himself to do the work of a slave?" Jesus picked up the towel and knelt before him. Peter cried, "Never, Lord. I will not allow You to wash my feet!" The calm voice of Jesus replied, "Peter, if I don't wash your feet, then you will not be a part of My work." Peter didn't yet understand why Jesus was washing his feet, but the fear of not being a part of the Master's work caused him to reconsider and to say, "Lord, wash my feet and also my hands and my head." Jesus smiled, "Peter My impetuous one, you do not need a bath." Peter perhaps wept softly as his friend poured the water over his feet and then gently wiped them dry with a towel. When Jesus had finished, He asked, "Do you understand why I have washed your feet? You call me your Lord and Master, and it is true. I am. But can you see that what I have done is for an example to you? If I, being your Lord and Master, am willing to be your servant, you who will represent Me to the world must also be a servant to mankind. If you will serve others, you will find happiness on earth." (See John 13:4-17.)

The above story about what might have been said as Jesus washed the disciples' feet is just one portion of the New Testament where Jesus taught a life of willing servitude. Jesus never advocated slavery, but rather, service in the kingdom of God. The Jews could not understand how this meek man, born of humble birth, could possibly be the promised Messiah who would restore Jerusalem and the Jewish nation as it had been in the golden days of Solomon. It quickly became apparent to them that this so-called Messiah named Jesus had not come to lead them in battle and victory against the mighty Roman Empire. Instead of war, He advocated love! His kingdom enlisted servants instead of soldiers. He taught that people should love their enemies and those who despitefully use them. They were ready for battle, but He talked about love—of turning the other cheek! He taught that people were to love their neighbors as themselves. He taught other principles of love and servitude, such as going two miles if a person asks you to go one, and giving our possessions to whomever asks to borrow them. He taught that if someone is hungry we should feed them. If someone needs clothes, clothe them. He even said that if someone offends you, forgive them; and if they offend you many times, you should forgive over and over again. In a parable found in Matthew 25:40, Jesus said, "Inasmuch as ye have done *it* unto one of the least of these my brethren, ye have done *it* unto me." So when we love or serve others, we are serving Him, and in service to Him, we will find happiness.

I once read that the atheist A. E. Houseman, professor at Cambridge University, spoke at Cambridge in 1936 on the subject "The Name and Nature of Poetry." He is quoted as saying, "The greatest truth ever uttered and the most profound moral discovery of all times were these words of Jesus: 'He that findeth his life shall lose it: and he that loseth his life for my sake shall find it.'" This pessimistic, atheistic, and allegedly suicidal man actually believed that the only way to find joy in life was to give oneself to others! And just as amazing are the words of another avowed atheist, Theodore Dreiser, who regarded life as "a tale told by an idiot, full of sound and fury, signifying nothing." But like Houseman, Dreiser prescribed the same antidote for unhappiness: service to others. Dreiser once said, "If man is to extract any joy out of his span, he must think and plan to make things better not only for himself but for others, since joy for himself depends upon his joy in others and theirs in him." If Houseman and Dreiser, self-proclaimed atheists, recognized that a life of servitude brings happiness, how much more should the children of God understand this basic principle?

Jesus taught by example and was a true model of servitude. He mingled among people from all walks of life, and His love for people was apparent as He healed the sick and opened blind eyes. Not showing partiality, He went to people where they were. He took an interest in the woman at the well and revealed to her the secret of eternal life. He didn't consider for even a moment that a Jew should not talk to a Samaritan woman. Jesus even ate supper with sinners and tax collectors. Because a person's station in life was not important to Jesus, He received great criticism from the Pharisees and the Sadducees. He wasn't concerned with what other people thought. He unconditionally loved all people. He came to save people from their sins. Jesus was a king, but He chose to serve!

Another great soulwinner and servant to the people was the apostle Paul. Paul was chosen of God perhaps because of his zeal to serve God. But before Paul could be used for the kingdom of God, God had to adjust Paul's attitude toward Christ and His followers. Paul was sincerely serving God—or so he thought—as he persecuted and killed Jews who followed Jesus Christ. As a devout Jew, Paul enforced the first and foremost law of God: "Hear, O Israel: The LORD our God *is* one LORD" (Deuteronomy 6:4). He just didn't understand that Jesus was God incarnate. Jesus revealed Himself to Paul on the road to Damascus. Paul's mission in life was forever changed when he recognized that Jesus was the one true God incarnate. After Paul realized who Jesus was, he humbly said, "Lord, what wilt thou have me to do?" (Acts 9:6). Paul led a life of servitude from that day forward. God first chose Paul, and then Paul chose to serve God, and by his own words, he did it for the gospel's sake: "For though I be free from all *men*, yet have I made myself servant unto all. . . . And this I do for the gospel's sake, that I might be partaker thereof with *you*" (I Corinthians 9:19, 23).

Like Paul, who was "made all things to all men," we must serve others. We may not have the same skills or the same personality, but each of us can be sensitive to the physical and spiritual needs of others. People are hurting. They have sought for peace and happiness in a world that dishes out discouragement and false hopes. As children of God, we have what they need, but we must first get people to realize that what they long for in life can only be found in Christ. Galileo said, "You cannot teach a man anything; you can only help him find it within himself."

Most sinners will not wake up one morning and think, "I need a savior;" but whether they realize it or not, they have an innate desire to know their Creator. The soul of man is weeping as Job wept, "Oh that I knew where I might find him!" (Job 23:3). That longing causes people to search for the Savior but often in all the wrong places. They fill their lives with what is tangible: entertainment, work, and materialism. They work harder and longer hours to buy newer and bigger homes. They fill these homes with expensive furniture and park new cars in the driveway. They travel the world or buy vacation homes. The bar, television, the golf course, the theater, or the bowling alley may fill their entertainment agenda. It is an endless bowing to materialism; and still, they search for that elusive butterfly of contentment.

As Jesus and the disciples served among the people, healing and making provision for them, the people learned to love them and were consequently ready to listen to the message of salvation. Similarly, we will win souls to Christ if we can first endear ourselves to others. We can do that by obeying the royal law (James 2:8) that says that we must love our neighbor as ourselves. This means that we must serve others, esteem others better than ourselves, and reach out to others in love and kindness. While the purpose in serving and loving others is so that we may win people to the kingdom of God, there is a two-fold benefit when we serve others: (1) They can see Christ in us; (2) The law of return goes into effect; that is, as we serve others, we reap happiness.

Sometimes, however, it is difficult to win the affection of some people. Through no fault of our own, sometimes people just don't like us. I always find these people to be a challenge to me. If at all possible, I like to get to the bottom of why they don't like me. It just makes sense that we can never win our enemy to Christ, so we must somehow gain their friendship. Once, as a teenager in high school, I received what I felt was undeserved disdain from a high school senior who was in the symphonic band with me. After symphony band tryouts, I was given a higher score than Brenda and was asked to sit in the clarinet section a few seats ahead of her. This senior was not happy about a freshman doing better than she! Brenda often glared at me and said mean things to me. I felt really uncomfortable around her but was determined to win her friendship. One day as I was telling some friends about my horses, an opportunity to win her friendship presented itself. Brenda overheard us talking, and I noticed how her face lit up. She even asked some questions about my horses. I took the opportunity to invite her to my house to ride with me. I could have been spiteful because of her attitude toward me or even lorded it over her because I was deemed a better clarinet player than she; but instead, I chose to share with Brenda my good fortune of owning horses. I chose the high road as I lowered myself to invite my self-proclaimed enemy to my house, to bridle and saddle a mount for her enjoyment, and to ride with her as if she were my best friend. Because I chose to love and serve her, I lost an enemy and gained a friend for life!

I have already mentioned how Jesus and Paul served in the kingdom of God, but there is another less familiar disciple who is remembered for leading people to Jesus: the apostle Andrew. Three times we read in the Gospels that Andrew led people to Jesus. The first time that Andrew met Jesus, he ran to find his brother, Peter, and cried, "We have found the Messiah." Andrew was excited that he had found the promised Messiah and wasn't a bit afraid about sharing Him with anyone who would listen. Later, Andrew brought the little lad with the loaves and fishes to Jesus. This boy was introduced to Jesus, shared his lunch, and went home with more bread and fish than he had brought. Andrew, along with Philip, also introduced some Greeks to Jesus. Apparently, Andrew showed no partiality between people. He knew that the gospel was for Gentiles as well as for Jews. What an example Andrew's discipleship is for us today! We must never lose our excitement about the hope that we have found in Jesus. The Spirit living within us is also the hope of our friends, family, and acquaintances. Like Andrew, I want to be known for bringing people to Jesus.

It really is not that hard to share Jesus with others. It should come naturally to born-again believers. We interact with people every day, and if we take the time to listen to them, they will give us opportunities to tell them about

Jesus. It doesn't matter what problems they face; Jesus is the answer. As consumers, when we find a product on the market that is everything the advertisers say, we tell our family and friends. We want to share the good deal with them. As children of God, we have found the product that no person or family can afford to be without. We must tell people that Jesus is everything we need. We have found Him to be our healer, our provider, our way-maker, our counselor, our savior, and so much more. He is a trustworthy, faithful God who cares about us. As a quality product, He comes with more than a lifetime guarantee—He is guaranteed faithful for all eternity!

We have what others need and can have. Salvation is not a commodity that can be bought or sold. Even if it could be, no one could afford it. It is priceless. Jesus paid for it with His own blood, and as the song says, "All to Him I owe." We can never repay Jesus for what He has done for us. But we can show our gratefulness by telling someone else about His saving grace. If we call ourselves servants of Christ, we must do what Jesus did. What Jesus did was sow the seed of the gospel. As servants we are laborers with God. Paul defined our job description this way: "I have planted, Apollos watered; but God gave the increase. So then neither is he that planteth any thing, neither he that watereth; but God that giveth the increase. . . . For we are labourers together with God" (I Corinthians 3:6, 9).

We are servants and sowers in the kingdom of God.

We are commissioned by Christ Himself to tell the lost about Him. Paul compared the spreading of the gospel to the sowing of seed. We sow the seed and then do whatever it takes for that seed to reach maturity. In the natural, a seed must be planted in fertile soil, watered, and given plenty of sunlight. In the spiritual, we pray for God to produce fertile ground in a sinner's heart, we sow the seed by revealing the plan of salvation, and water that soul with the love of God. Just as weeds begin to grow around a new plant and must be pulled to prevent them from choking out the plant, newborns in Christ must be tended to make sure the cares of this life do not choke them before they reach maturity in Christ. The command to sow, therefore, involves more than just sowing the seed. A farmer doesn't just sow the seed and then let the garden come up on its own. Just as there are many steps in raising crops to reach maturity, a sinner from repentance to maturity needs the help of the church. It doesn't mean that one person necessarily has to fulfill all the steps. Paul said that one sows, one waters, and God gives the increase. And so the church grows, one soul at a time.

I have often heard people say that they prefer a small church. This never made any sense to me, because churches that are not growing are often churches that are not obeying the command of Jesus. A healthy church is a growing church.

From the dawn of Creation, God set His law of reproduction in motion. We read about it in the Book of

Genesis. God made everything to reproduce after its kind, and man is not an exception. After God created Adam and Eve, He commanded them to "be fruitful, and multiply" (Genesis 1:28). Spiritually speaking, Christians are also to be fruitful and multiply, or to reproduce after their kind. More simply, Christians are to produce Christians.

Here is how the law of reproduction works: When one grain of corn is planted, it could conceivably produce as many as one thousand grains of corn per year. If every grain that is produced is planted and that process is repeated with each yield of the crops, in just six years, the whole world would be planted in corn! Planting the seed of the gospel is similar in principle. If every Christian would tell just one person about God's love, and that person tells one, and that person tells one, just think how quickly the gospel would multiply!

As I have mentioned many times already, once the power of the Holy Spirit begins to work within us, we begin to sow the gospel seed. The first thing that happens after our conversion is that people immediately notice that we have changed. I have heard it said over and over again that, when a person returns to work after being filled with the Holy Spirit, fellow employees notice the change and want to know what happened. Familiar comments are, "What happened to you? There is something different about you this morning." What an opportunity to share how Jesus saved us. We don't even have to think about how to share the gospel. God's Spirit has started His work, and we don't even realize that we are already on assignment for the kingdom.

Our testimony, our words, and our actions sow seeds of faith. We are not an island, but everything that we say and do does affect those who are around us. It is okay to rejoice in the presence of a sinner about what a great experience we have had in God or about the wonderful church service on Sunday. People begin to consider their need for God when we tell them how someone was miraculously healed. I know because it happened to me. Before I was saved, I remember my cousin, Loretta, telling me about how God spared her life when she was a teenager. I remember her praying over a dying baby duck and seeing that duck come back to life. I remember well her faith in God. My own faith began to grow each time I heard a testimonial of God's great power.

As we allow the Spirit of God to work within us, we develop a reputation for being a person of faith. People will remember our faces when they have a need. I have had many people call me on the telephone or e-mail asking me to pray for them. A good Catholic neighbor of mine often said to me, "God hears you when you pray; would you please pray that God would (fill in the blank)?"

Doors of opportunity open if we are good listeners when people need to pour out their troubles. We may not know how to mend a broken marriage or to repair a dysfunctional family, but we do know the One who can.

The only requirement for sharing Christ is to have an ongoing relationship with Him so that we can tell others that we trust Jesus and have found Him to be the answer to every need.

As Christ's witnesses, we must talk the talk and walk the walk. In other words, we cannot be hypocritical. There is an old saying: "What you are speaks so loudly I cannot hear what you say." We must live our lives in Christ in such a manner that this saying is changed to: "What you are speaks so loudly that I must pay attention to what you say." We will destroy our witness if we don't live victoriously and above reproach at all times. We should live in such a manner that others will see our victorious lives. People are looking for hope and something different from what the world has to offer. At all times, we should reflect Christ's loveliness, His grace, and His ability to change lives.

After we have gained the friendship and trust of a person, then we can invite them to church or offer to teach them a Bible study. I know that some of you are thinking right about now that you might be able to reflect Christ to others through your lifestyle, but you doubt if you have the ability to teach a Bible study. No doubt I thought the same thing years ago when I was presented with my first opportunity to teach a Bible study. We begin forming excuses in our minds the same as Moses when he was called to deliver the children of Israel from Egyptian bondage.

Moses' calling is such an interesting study and reveals so much about the nature of mankind. When God gave Moses his first assignment, Moses questioned his qualifications to be a deliverer. He said to God, "Who *am* I, that I should go unto Pharaoh, and that I should bring forth the children of Israel out of Egypt?" (Exodus 3:11). God patiently tried to assure Moses that He would be there to help him. Still not convinced, Moses questioned his credibility with the people. "But, behold, they will not believe me, nor hearken unto my voice: for they will say, The LORD hath not appeared unto thee" (Exodus 4:1). When that excuse didn't work with God, Moses used one more defense for his fear to face Pharaoh. He simply said that he didn't have a knack for public speaking. Although God repeatedly assured Moses that He would mold him into the needed utensil of the Lord, Moses was not to be persuaded and finally asked the Lord to send someone else, thus provoking the anger of God. God then told Moses that He knew that Aaron could speak well and therefore chose Aaron to be the speaker instead of Moses. Because of Moses' unwillingness to be pliable in God's hands, he became part of God's permissive will, rather than his perfect will. God's plan was modified slightly: God would speak to Moses, who would tell Aaron what to say to Pharaoh.

How many times does God want to use us in a specific way, but because of our lack of faith, we miss His perfect will? Just like Moses, we sometimes argue with

God: "I have a difficult time explaining things. I will bore people to death. I'm afraid to talk in front of people." And finally the clincher, "There are people more qualified than I to teach a Bible study." When fear grips our hearts, we can come up with a multitude of excuses. If Moses, the greatest prophet of the Old Testament, could stand before God and make up excuses, then it is okay for you and me to duck the will of God, right? No, of course not! Moses actually angered God, but God, knowing that Moses had the ability, did not completely let him off the hook. Moses did become a deliverer; and you and I, because of God's Spirit living within us, are ordained to win others to Christ. His Spirit assures us that we will be witnesses. It is true that some will become more proactive than others. It is not a question of whether or not we will be witnesses for Christ, but rather how successful we will become in soulwinning.

I am not sure why God chose Moses to deliver the children of Israel out of Egypt, but I am confident that Moses was chosen of God even before the day of his birth. Perhaps God's confidence in Moses stemmed from the fact that He saw how much Moses loved Israel, the people of his nationality. The Book of Hebrews says that Moses "refused to be called the son of Pharaoh's daughter; Choosing rather to suffer affliction with the people of God, than to enjoy the pleasures of sin for a season" (Hebrews 11:24-25). Whatever the reason God chose Moses, we know that God is sovereign and uses whomever He desires to perform His will. If God calls us to teach a Bible study, our attitude should be, "If God says I am able, that settles it; I can do it!"

All across the United States, churches are bursting at the seams. New church structures and larger sanctuaries are in the planning stages or are being built. Empty pews are longing to be filled. Many souls are waiting to hear the gospel. Today is the day to dismiss doubt and fear about our abilities and partner ourselves with the Holy Spirit within us. What a day to serve and to sow that others may hear the gospel!

CHAPTER FOUR

Techniques for Soulwinning

It really doesn't matter how we win the lost to Christ, because He didn't command any particular method. What He did say is that He would give us power to witness. There are different methods to win the lost. Some people have a knack for bringing people to Christ with their ability to explain the plan of salvation; others are good at giving their testimony, while still others live their testimony. Paul said, "Ye are our epistle written in our hearts, known and read of all men" (II Corinthians 3:2).

I can't stress enough that if we are going to win folks to Christ, we must live what we believe at all times because people are watching us. I recall sitting at a mother-daughter banquet beside a visitor, who began to stare at our pastor's wife as she walked past us. This woman said to me, "That lady glows with the Spirit of God." People scrutinize Christians because they want to know if Christ really makes a difference. It is a fact that most people want to know that a product works before purchasing it. I don't think it is any different with the gospel of Christ. If people see that Christ has made a difference in our lives, they are more likely to listen to what we have to say about the gospel. Many times people have come to me and said, "I can tell that you are a Christian." I know that this has happened to many children of God, and this is as it should be. We should stand out in the crowd. If people can't see Christ in us, then we are doing something wrong!

In this chapter, I shall give several general principles or techniques to guide you in soulwinning, with the hope that by learning them—and applying them—you will become a confident soulwinner for Christ.

For whatever you want to learn how to do, someone has written a how-to handbook about it. Childbirth is a good example since there are many similarities between natural and spiritual childbirth. When a couple discovers that they are expecting a child, they often look for a handbook on birthing. First-time parents usually want to learn all they can before the birth of their child because there is a certain fear about what is to take place; and knowledge dispels fear. Similarly, learning a few techniques on how to win souls will dispel the fear of witnessing or teaching Bible studies. As I have indicated in the title of this book, we are not alone in the birthing process. Just as a mother depends on her coach or the medical staff during childbirth, so the child of God depends on the Holy Spirit in soulwinning. The Spirit's power within will help us and will often even teach us what we should say.

When I began to witness and teach Bible studies, I read everything I could about how to share the gospel. I also attended church growth seminars. This gave me confidence, but experience proved to be the best teacher. I assume that since you are reading this book, you have a burden for lost souls. But if you don't have a burden (and know that you should), ask God for it. If you feel that you lack wisdom or ability, ask God for wisdom, and He will give it to you (James 1:5). God is able to anoint and strengthen our natural talents and abilities. Be assured that He delights in making us into useful vessels. If you truly have a desire to win souls, ask the Lord to make you a soulwinner. Jesus said, "Follow me, and I will make you fishers of men" (Matthew 4:19).

When I think about God's ability to make us into useful vessels for His kingdom, I recall how He gave supernatural wisdom to the children of Israel to build the Tabernacle in the wilderness. The magnificence of the Tabernacle required skills far beyond the natural abilities of those Israelites. After God had given detailed instructions to Moses on how to make the intricately carved furniture, the curtained walls, the utensils, and even the clothes that the priests were to wear, God told Moses,

"Speak unto all *that are* wise hearted, whom I have filled with the spirit of wisdom" (Exodus 28:3). God gave them wisdom to build that beautiful Tabernacle. If God gave them wisdom to build a place where people could come into His presence in the Old Testament, how much more will He grant wisdom to those who desire to be soulwinners? Don't underestimate your abilities as Moses did his, but believe that with God all things are possible. And if you still doubt your abilities, repeat after Paul, "I can do all things through Christ which strengtheneth me" (Philippians 4:13). We do not have to fear rejection or inability, because Christ has endued us with power through His Spirit within. He will encourage and strengthen us as we share His gospel with lost souls. Now, let us look at a few techniques and personal examples that will help in soulwinning.

Make Contacts

Keep in mind that we each have our own unique circle of friends and acquaintances. Our differences in circumstances will lead to a variety of potential people with whom we may share the gospel. Your first contact may be a co-worker or someone in your family. Perhaps you will witness to a cashier at the grocery store or a bank teller. Your neighborhood is a perfect place for soulwinning. Wherever you are or whatever your unique circumstances happen to be, always keep your eyes open for opportunities to witness to those whose path God has allowed you to cross.

This might seem too easy, but one really effective place to make contacts and witness is at church. First, within our churches is a group of people that we might easily overlook: people who come regularly to church and may even consider themselves "members" of the church, but who have, nevertheless, not been born again. We might just assume they are saved because they have been attending the church for a long time. These folks may have been baptized but have never received the Holy Spirit for various reasons—they are "partially born babies." Even though some have attended church a long time, they still may have never understood the plan of salvation and are waiting for someone to show them. God forbid that people in our own pews will be lost just because we did not reach out to them after seeing their need! Be sensitive to those who may be in this situation, and ask God to help you befriend them. Once you have befriended them, chances are they will allow you to share the Word with them and lead them to full salvation.

Second, more than likely, there will be new visitors at our churches each week. Before each service, I look for visitors, shake their hands, and attempt to strike up a conversation with them. As we become a conduit of God's love to a visitor, they are actually seeing Jesus in us. When visitors come through our church doors, we must be sure to shake their hands and be friendly. When we shake a hand, we may melt a heart and create a lifetime friend. In this manner of sharing God's love, I have made many friends. Once the door of friendship is opened, it is easy then to share the gospel.

Have Good Interpersonal Skills

I want to stress what I just mentioned above. There are some qualities that we must possess in order to endear ourselves to people, whether we are witnessing in the church or outside the church. For example, we must be friendly and smile at people. There is nothing more beautiful and relaxing as a smile. People who don't smile make me nervous. A frowning face causes me to think that I have done something wrong, whereas a smile puts me at ease. Most important of all, a smile is one way that people can see Jesus in us.

If we wear a smile instead of a frown,
We can turn lost sinners completely around.
For Jesus gives us a joy in our heart,
That when we smile, His love we impart.
DMK

Becoming a good listener is another quality that we must develop. It goes hand in hand with being friendly. Publilius Syrus, a Roman poet born one hundred years before Christ, said, "We are interested in others when they are interested in us." It is human nature to like people who like us. If we will listen to what people are saying and take an interest in what they are doing, they may open up to us and hear what we have to say concerning the gospel of Christ and the salvation of their souls. If there is one thing that our world is short on, it is people who really listen to what others are saying. Most of the time, we are so concerned about what we are going to say that we don't hear what they are trying to say. Sinners have problems. If you listen carefully, you will pick up on their needs. You have the answer to their problems, but they will never trust you if you do not gain their confidence. And you will never gain their confidence if you do not listen to them. People want to be heard. Even the Bible encourages good listening, "Wherefore, my beloved brethren, let every man be swift to hear, slow to speak, slow to wrath" (James 1:19). So be friendly and listen to people, and you will gain their confidence. Then, more than likely, they will tell you about their family difficulties, broken relationships, concern for the economy or even for the depraved condition of our world. This will naturally lead to an opportunity for you to tell them about Jesus.

Find Common Ground

As you greet people in church, on the street, or wherever you meet, strike up a conversation, and look for something you may have in common. I call this "finding common ground." I love to talk to people and am always amazed at the things we have in common. Sometimes I ask where they live and try to think about something I know about that area. Perhaps their name sounds familiar so I may ask if they know someone I know. Surprisingly, they often do know the person I mention. I am convinced that God has already arranged our meeting.

One time I spoke to a woman who was visiting a special service at our church. I asked her where she was from and her reply was, "Cambridge, Ohio, which is about a two-hour drive." I remarked that my father was born and raised there. I told her my father's name and she said, "Well, the only Unklesbay that I know from Cambridge was a young, expectant mother who died from pneumonia on her way to the hospital in the late 1920s. The woman and her baby both died." She was referring to my father's sister, and while I was surprised to learn that she knew of my aunt's death, I was not surprised that she related something about my family since we are the only Unklesbays who came to America from Holland. How quickly and miraculously I had found common ground with a stranger! Another time, I greeted a visitor who said she was from Marshallville, Ohio. I paused for a moment to surf my memory banks and then said, "The only thing I know about Marshallville is that our veterinarian lived there." I mentioned old Doc Feeney's name, and not only did she know the man, but she informed me that he had retired and his son had taken over the business. Again, I had found common ground. I don't understand how God brings about such meetings, but I do believe that He does it when we desire to win people to Christ. If we can find common ground with people, we are well on our way to establishing a rapport with them, which in turn could lead to an opportunity to witness.

Turn Conversations toward God, Church, or Religion

As soon as possible in any conversation, try to get the subject turned to church, God, or religion. Since our lives are centered around the church, that is usually not a difficult thing to do. I often bring the conversation around to the things of God by mentioning how my children are involved in ministry or Bible quizzing. These facts always get people's attention. They usually will ask me where I go to church. When I tell them that I go to a Pentecostal or apostolic church, I am always amazed when an individual tells me that they know someone from my church or other people who are Pentecostal. Often, people tell me that they come from a Pentecostal background. As I have already said, I don't believe very much in coincidence, so I am convinced that God's Spirit has already set the groundwork for our meeting.

If you're not sure how to get a conversation turned to church, don't be afraid to ask them if they have a religious belief or go to church. Ask them about their beliefs, but never, never, never put down their belief or church! It is better to build on rather than to destroy what they know and believe about God. Regardless of how you direct the conversation toward God or church or religion, remember that the Holy Spirit is at work in the process as well—He's waiting to speak through you, so don't get stressed about what you are going to say! The important thing is to take the time to develop friendships and to allow the Spirit of God to work through you.

Share Testimonies

A good way to get people's attention is to share our testimony or maybe the testimony of someone else. We can also tell people about a miracle that has taken place in our church services or somewhere in the world. This will make them curious about our church and its beliefs. When talking about miracles, we should not neglect to mention the greatest of all miracles: our salvation! I like to hear about miracles, but I do not regard any miracle as more important than the miracle of salvation. Also, I am fully aware that miracles are blessings to all mankind and not just to saints. Sometimes God heals or provides for sinners—I believe so that they may recognize God's hand in situations and perhaps even find Him.

I often tell people how good God has been to me. I tell them that God has healed my body numerous times. I testify that God has never failed to provide financially for my family. However, I also make clear that my faith is the same whether or not God heals, makes provision, or performs miracles in my life. I tell them that, in all things,

God's grace is sufficient for me and that I accept His will for my life and serve Him because He is sovereign—not because He does things for me.

Memorize Key Scriptures

While you don't have to be a Bible scholar or know a lot of Scripture to be a soulwinner, sometimes you may feel more confident if you know a few key scriptures. Pastor Garry Tracy of New Life Pentecostal Church in Bridgeton, Missouri, gave his congregation four scriptures that are good to know when leading a sinner to Christ. They are as follows:

- "For all have sinned, and come short of the glory of God" (Romans 3:23).
- "For God so loved the world, that he gave his only begotten Son, that whosoever believeth in him should not perish, but have everlasting life" (John 3:16).
- "Marvel not that I said unto thee, Ye must be born again" (John 3:7).
- "Then Peter said unto them, Repent, and be baptized every one of you in the name of Jesus Christ for the remission of sins, and ye shall receive the gift of the Holy Ghost" (Acts 2:38).

The first verse causes people to acknowledge that they are a sinner. This is not a comfortable feeling, so quickly give them the second verse, which replaces utter despair with hope in knowing that, although they are a sinner, God loves sinners and gave His Son to die for them. Then have them read the command of Jesus that says we must be born again, followed by how to be born again in Acts 2:38. In just four scriptures, people may discover their sin and learn immediately how to remedy their sinful situation.

Offer to Teach a Home Bible Study

Once you have developed a rapport with people, tell them that you teach home Bible studies, and ask if they would be interested in going through one with you. (The next chapter deals in greater depth with teaching home Bible studies.) I usually mention that I teach a longer study that takes about twelve weeks, but that I also have two condensed studies: one that takes one hour and the other, two hours, which is divided into two days.

People often tell me that they don't understand how to read the Bible or that they just don't understand the Bible. I quickly inform them that the Bible is not a great mystery and that anyone can learn to read it with a little guidance. I emphasize that all of us need to learn from someone who has studied the Scriptures. I also inform them that the longer Bible study will help them learn more about reading their Bible and will briefly outline everything contained in the Bible from Genesis to Revelation. Depending on their spiritual background, I often explain that God opens the Scripture up enough for people to get saved and then gives more understanding once they have received the Holy Spirit.

As we attempt to secure a Bible study, we should explain that we are concerned for their time and will not take any more than one hour a week. We may offer to teach in their home, our home, or a neutral place, such as the church. We should get their name, address, phone number, and set up a time for the study. If they are not sure that they want to do a study, we should give them our name and phone number. We need to be careful not to pressure them. If we make them angry, we may not be given another chance to ask. Perhaps later they will change their mind. One lady turned me down the first time I asked but came back to the church after a few months and specifically looked me up to see if I would still teach her.

We must also never pressure people into coming to our churches. In fact, when you are talking to them about doing a Bible study with you, assure them that you will not pressure them into coming to church. Give God time to speak to their hearts. You may invite them to a service over the course of time now and then, but don't ever pressure them. Look for special services, such as at Easter or Christmas when most people feel a certain obligation to go to church.

But if or when they do come to church, be sensitive to them. For example, people who come alone often appreciate it when you sit with them or introduce them to someone else in the church who will be friendly to them. However, always respect their desires. Some will want to sit by themselves, while others will greatly appreciate your offer to sit with them. When you seat them, ask where they would like to sit because some visitors feel very uncomfortable sitting at the front of the church and others will feel left out if you seat them too far back.

Another way to win points with your visitors if they bring their children is to speak kindly to their children and offer to take them to the appropriate Sunday school class. Again, be sensitive to your visitors' desires and don't be overaggressive. If children are clinging to their mom or dad, ask nicely if they would like to go to class. If they don't want to, act as if that is perfectly fine. Some children require a few weeks coming to the church before they are comfortable to leave their parents. Above all, you want your visitors to be comfortable.

While soulwinning is not difficult, it is not for the fainthearted. It is not for the one who throws in the towel at the first sign of rejection. It will require rolled-up sleeves and a determination to do all that is possible to lead a soul to Christ.

And remember that, while the purpose of our sharing the gospel is not to be blessed, we do, in fact, receive blessings when souls are saved. This is another example of God's law of return. "Cast thy bread upon the waters: for thou shalt find it after many days" (Ecclesiastes 11:1). As we witness and share God's love, blessings will return pressed down so that there will not be room enough to receive it! There is great joy and benefits in soulwinning.

Summary of Techniques for Soulwinning

- Make contacts wherever you are.
- Have good interpersonal skills.
- Strike up a conversation and find common ground.
- When talking to people, turn the subject to church, God, or religion.
- Share testimonies.
- Memorize a few key scriptures to get people thinking about their soul.
- Tell people that you teach Bible studies and offer to teach them one.

CHAPTER FIVE

Home Bible Studies

I noted in the last chapter that, after building rapport with sinners, you should offer to teach them a home Bible study. In my experience, teaching home Bible studies has been the single most effective way to win people to the Lord and to establish them in the truth. (I especially believe in the value of home Bible studies since my husband and I were led to a full understanding of God's Word through the *Search for Truth* home Bible study!) In this chapter, I shall focus on how to use home Bible studies effectively to win the lost.

As mentioned earlier, we are witnesses for Christ—for good or bad—through our lifestyles as people observe our behavior. While we should live our testimony before people at all times, there is also a need to verbally share Christ. Some people are naturally good at talking to others about the plan of salvation. Some folks like myself need or want a tool to help them share the gospel. This is where home Bible studies play an important role. There are so many different kinds of studies that I believe almost anyone could use them as a tool to share the gospel.

Bible Study Options

You have a couple of basic options for home Bible studies: one-hour or two-hour studies and ten-week or twelve-week studies. You may want to try one of the shorter ones first, but don't limit yourself to those. You will learn so much more from the longer studies.

The one-hour or two-hour studies are user-friendly. Just about anyone can teach with these fully prepared studies. Basically, the shorter studies set the stage for an immediate decision concerning salvation by asking questions that are answered by reading verses of Scripture. As you teach, I recommend purchasing two of the study booklets, one for you, the teacher, and one for the student. Because these lessons are designed so that just about anyone can teach a Bible study, all you have to do is read the question and have the student read the scripture to answer the question. When the student reads the scripture, it speaks to the student's heart and leaves no room for argument. One word of caution: you should have studied well enough to have answers ready if the student has difficulty filling in the blank. Of course, most students will understand the scripture and can easily answer the questions without our assistance. Because I keep my booklet as a study guide to be used over and over, I already have the answers filled in.

Again, the shorter studies' simplicity makes them ideal for most people to teach. I have found the one-hour study *Into His Marvelous Light* to be particularly useful. (This study and several like it are available through Word Aflame Press, Hazelwood, MO.) My church, in fact, teaches *Into His Marvelous Light* to every individual who is baptized. Besides helping a new convert understand the plan of salvation or what they may have experienced at the altar, it becomes an excellent teaching tool for the new convert to take home and share with unsaved family members.

In addition to these shorter studies, I have frequently used ten-week and twelve-week studies. Each study is a valuable tool, but if your goal is to develop a long-term relationship, the longer studies are the most appropriate. One excellent twelve-week Bible study that I recommend for beginners and most teachers is *Exploring God's Word*. I like this particular study because it is easy to read and is limited in the amount of material you read each week to prepare for the lesson. My personal favorite, however, is another twelve-week study called *Search for Truth II*. This study has a lot of reading material. It is a Bible course in itself! If you use this study, you will need to be able to condense the material in order to keep each lesson confined to a one-hour maximum. Both *Exploring God's Word* and *Search For Truth II* are well written and similar in content. Both are excellent. Their beautifully illustrated charts are similar as well. The charts come in two sizes: The large chart is 15" by 20" and is large enough for a group of people to see from a distance, and the other is 8½" by 11" for use with one or two people sitting at a table. (Both of these Bible studies are available through Word Aflame Press, Hazelwood, MO.)

I often use more than one study with a student, especially if I feel I need more time to bring my student to a decision to serve Christ. If you are not sure which study to use, you may want to talk to your Bible study coordinator in your church or your pastor to help you choose which study would be appropriate. Representatives at Word Aflame Press can also be consulted about their Bible studies.

Preparing to Teach

To become an effective Bible study teacher, you will need to keep the following four key points in mind as you prepare to teach: (1) Be filled with God's Spirit. (2) Pray and ask God to make you into a skillful teacher. (3) Purchase a good Bible study and practice teaching it. (4) Ask God to send a soul for you to teach.

The first point in preparing to teach a Bible study should be obvious by this time. You must be filled with the power of God's Spirit. You cannot teach truth unless the Truth lives within you. The second point is that before you ever begin any project for the Lord (and this should be obvious), you must pray and ask God to make you into a skillful teacher. Also, before you teach a study or attempt to tell someone about the gospel, ask the Lord to give you direction. A soul is at stake. No matter how competent you get in handling the Word of God, you need the anointing of the Holy Spirit. God is faithful and will guide you "by the skillfulness of his hands" (Psalm 78:72).

The third point in preparing to teach a home Bible study is to purchase a good study and practice teaching. God will do His part to make you a good teacher only if you do your part and prepare yourself. Teaching using carefully researched studies is an effective tool to share the gospel. There are excellent home Bible studies that practically teach themselves. Nonetheless, the study will go so much better if you have put the time in to be thoroughly familiar with the study—and this can only come from practice.

Finally, ask God to open a door of opportunity. Specifically, ask Him to send someone into your life who needs a Bible study. By faith, it will happen because it is God's will to reach the lost. I found that I had more studies than I could keep up with after I prayed such a prayer. If that happens, don't be afraid to ask the pastor or Bible study coordinator of your church to find someone to help you teach. You do not want to burn yourself out or schedule more than you can handle. By asking someone else to teach a study, you allow them to become a blessing to someone else.

After you pray, be prepared to do your part. People won't just come to you out of nowhere and ask if you teach Bible studies. There is an old saying, "Prayer needs hands and feet." You take one step, and God will take two. Or more simply, you do your part and God will do His. So pray and then keep alert for the opportunity to teach a Bible study. Besides these four key points, there are several other practical guidelines to follow in order to teach successful Bible studies.

Protect Your and Your Students' Reputation

You must always protect your reputation and your students' reputations by teaching people of the same gender or by bringing along another person to be in the room with you as you teach. My husband and I teach Bible studies together when we are teaching another couple or a member of the opposite gender. It is never proper for a woman to be alone with a man or for a man to be alone with a woman, not even when teaching the Word of God. Using some common sense when dealing with the opposite gender will eliminate any chance of gossip and will keep you and your students above reproach.

Pray and Fast

As you prepare for the first Bible study lesson, remember that you must make a good impression or you may not be invited back. So, the week before your first lesson, pray and fast. Jesus, the greatest teacher who ever lived, prayed and fasted forty days in the wilderness before beginning His ministry. He prayed all night before choosing the twelve men who would become His apostles. If Jesus, "in the days of his flesh" (Hebrews 5:7), prayed for God's will and guidance, we should follow His example. We need God's anointing as we open the Word of God to our students' understanding. Pray also that as you teach and spend time with your students, you will be able to discover their needs and what sins keep them bound. Your goal is to teach the Word that will both reveal their sin and set them free from it at the same time. God will reveal to you their needs, so never underestimate the power of prayer and fasting.

Begin and End the Bible Study with Prayer

Always begin and end your Bible study with prayer. If you have brought a partner, one of you should pray before beginning the lesson. Do not embarrass your student by asking him to pray. When I teach, I usually say the prayer, or if my husband or another saint has accompanied me to the Bible study, I may ask him or her to pray, but rarely do I ask a student to pray. There are exceptions. If your students have been in church and consider themselves Christian, ask if they would like to pray over the lesson. People who believe themselves to be right with God may become offended if you do not ask them to pray. Keep in mind that some students really love God and are living by all they understand. As a teacher, our purpose is to build on what they already know, not to alienate them by questioning their experience in God. If your students, regardless of spiritual background, ask to pray, by all means allow them to pray over the lesson. This boosts their confidence and increases their faith.

Hold Questions, if Possible, until the End of the Lesson

Ask your students to hold most questions until the end of the lesson. Be flexible because some questions must be answered immediately. If you allow the question, don't be afraid to say that you will answer that particular question in a later lesson if they can wait. You will never get through your lesson if you allow constant interruptions. And I can't overemphasize the need to stay within the one-hour limit. Also, don't be afraid to tell them that you don't know the answer to a question. Write the question down and reassure them that you will find the answer for them. Then be sure to follow through and bring the answer to the next lesson.

Make Your Students Comfortable

When you begin teaching, whether at your home, the church, or in their home, make sure that you and your students are comfortable. If you are teaching the longer studies, you will need a place to set up your chart. I usually like to teach around a table. Everyone is seated including the teacher, and it makes for a more relaxed atmosphere. Incidentally, if your student has children, you might consider bringing a baby-sitter to prevent interruptions.

Do Not Read or Memorize the Lesson

Never read the lesson or memorize it word for word. Reading the lesson sends the message that you are not prepared or that you really don't know your subject. Memorizing may give you a monotone or canned sound. It is better to write down some brief notes on paper or index cards if there is something you particularly want to remember. The charts will prompt your memory on what to say next.

Limit the Number of Scriptures Read

Don't read too many verses of Scripture. There are many scriptures on the charts, but don't feel like you have to read all of them. Time will not permit reading too many of them. Also, teachers have different thoughts on who should read the scriptures. I play it by ear. Sometimes it is good for the teacher to read the scriptures for three reasons: (1) You are trying to stay within a time limit; (2) Reading the scriptures keeps you in control of the study; and (3) Until you know your students well, you do not want to embarrass them if they are poor readers. Sometimes students will ask to read. If that is the case, then by all means allow them to help with some of the reading. There are some scriptures, especially in the New Testament, that I always ask my students to read if they are able because I want those particular scriptures to speak directly to their hearts. Some of those scriptures are those that teach salvation or perhaps holy living. Always encourage your students to look up scriptures that you simply do not have time for in a one-hour lesson after the lesson is over.

Don't Give Too Much Information

Don't try to give too much information. You will study a lot more than you will teach. Some home Bible study teacher's manuals have an overwhelming amount of information. Study it to be prepared to answer questions; but again, don't overload students' minds with too much information. If you say too much, you might inspire topics that a seeker or new convert does not need to deal with right then. Our pastor always taught that when the Bible is silent on a subject, we should also remain silent. Your main topic should always stay on salvation. Above all, don't wear out your students by going too long! You want to leave them wanting more, not wondering how to get rid of you!

Give Your Students Handouts

It is a good idea to have a handout. A handout might be an outline of the topic discussed or a list of the scriptures to be read or both. *Search for Truth II* comes with a student handout, which is an outline of what the lesson covers and includes the scriptures to be read. Between sessions, encourage your students to study the outline and the scriptures listed. Some students might even be interested in purchasing one of the colorful, smaller charts to either *Search for Truth II* or *Exploring God's Word.* If they are interested, be sure to help them place an order for one.

Make Your Lessons Interesting

Make your lesson interesting, as well as informative. Make it exciting! The following are some suggestions: Communicate in a warm, friendly, and relaxed manner. Use appropriate hand gestures, voice fluctuations, and facial expressions. A monotone voice will bore your students. Bring in cassette tapes and newspaper articles. Don't be afraid to use object lessons. Be a good storyteller. For example, the story of Noah's ark doesn't have to be redundant. You can really get creative in telling about how the people outside of the ark might have been screaming in anguish as the floodwaters rose. You might scrape your nails on a blackboard to emphasize the people's terror as they tried to open the closed door of the ark. Look for and bring in some interesting articles from magazines and newspapers concerning archeological discoveries of the ark in our century. Be creative and make old stories relevant to your student.

Show How the Bible Is Relevant for Today

Every lesson has a spiritual application and is relevant to our lives. The Bible is an ageless document, so when you teach, don't just repeat the biblical material and explain what it meant then; show how it applies today. Help your students understand that Bible characters faced the same problems and temptations that we face and had similar experiences that we have. For example, point out that, like Adam and Eve, when we sin, we feel guilty and often "hide" from God. Explain that we have the same sinful nature as these ancestors. Like Adam and Eve, we don't like to admit our guilt, even when our hand is caught in the proverbial cookie jar. And we don't like to take responsibility for our actions, so we frequently blame someone else, like Adam, who blamed Eve, who in turn blamed the serpent.

Stress the Need for Personal Salvation

Until our students understand that they are sinners, they will not seek God's grace. Lesson after lesson reveals man's fallen nature and encourages students that, just as God forgave the people in the Bible, He will forgive us when we turn to Him in obedient faith, trusting in Christ alone for salvation. When you tell people that God in His mercy substituted His Son for an animal sacrifice, you give them an escape route from sin. As you tell story after story of man's failures and God's mercy, what you are really doing is offering hope. You show them that problems have solutions. You also give them a choice, they can choose to serve God or go back to the world. In every lesson, these timeless issues point the way toward God's plan of salvation. As you teach from week to week, you give your students the opportunity to acknowledge their sin and seek a place of repentance. Again, remember, sin is bondage and all sinners are in bondage to something: to their jobs, themselves, alcohol, drugs, cigarettes, and, yes, even to their churches. During your Bible study, you must become a friend and genuinely interested in others and willing to bring them to their crisis or to that which keeps them from God. After you can bring them to their crisis and help them through it, you can then lead them to God.

Be Informed of World News for Teaching Bible Prophecy

Know what is happening in world news because it is very relevant to Bible prophecy. Prophecy is something that is encountered throughout the Word of God and is not just a subject to be addressed as you teach Daniel or the Book of Revelation. For example, you will teach in one of the earlier lessons of some studies that the first prophecy concerning the coming of Jesus is actually found in the first book of the Bible. (See Genesis 3:15.)

In the longer home Bible studies, there are lessons on end-time prophecy. During these lessons, I often suggest that, after we have finished our twelve-week course, if they are interested in learning more about end-time prophecy, they can study Irvin Baxter's *Understanding The End-Time* Prophecy course. (There are, of course, other resources for this topic besides Irvin Baxter's, but I'm familiar with his and know that it is a good study on prophecy. Help your student, if asked, to find other resources for further study.) Irvin Baxter's course can be taught or watched on video tape. It is good to watch the tapes with your students so that you can answer questions that may come up. It may also be appropriate to lend the tapes to them during the weeks that you are teaching the ten-week or twelve-week Bible study. Again, when you are dealing with people, remember that every individual is different and so will your approach be to your student's needs.

Reschedule Canceled Lessons as Soon as Possible

If for some reason you or your students must cancel a lesson, be sure to reschedule as soon as possible. Try not to allow more than a week to pass. If there is a problem with the time that you have chosen, find out if there is a better time. Be flexible. You may have to change the day or time of a study from week to week. Be sensitive to the needs of your students, lest they get discouraged and quit because they "just don't have the time."

Love and Befriend Your Students

Determine to make this person a friend. Love your students. Sometimes it is hard to love the unlovable. If you find it difficult to love sinners, spend some time in I Corinthians 13. Love endures all things. Love is patient. Love is kind. Read this chapter until it becomes a part of you. Never act like you are in a hurry. Listen carefully and show that you are interested in what they are saying. I have said it before, but it bears repeating: people need someone to hear what they are saying. They aren't looking for a great deal of advice, and they don't need to hear about your problems. Listen carefully and talk very little about yourself. But above all, be sensitive to the Holy Spirit and depend on His help in loving your students.

Don't Argue

Refuse to argue. Show your students what the Word says and let the Word speak for itself. I have complete confidence that the Holy Spirit speaks to our students' hearts during the lessons. If you stay with the lesson plan, you should not get into controversial issues. It is possible that you will get into some controversy if some of your students have a strong background in another denomination and are familiar with the Bible. In this situation, it is critical not to argue with them. Lovingly—but firmly—direct them to the appropriate scriptures. We must always gently show people the truth using wisdom. For example, if some of your students say that they are already saved, do not deny their experience. You might say something along these lines, "I know that you love the Lord, but if God has more for you, wouldn't you want to know it?" Then go back to the scriptures that reveal what they need.

The Bible must always be the sole authority on every topic. And remember that you have truth on your side! Also, as I said before, if the Bible is silent on a subject, then we need to be silent. There could be nothing worse than to argue with your students about non-essential issues that are not clearly and directly addressed in Scripture.

Don't Get Angry

Above all, never get angry. Listen carefully so that you know what they are trying to say. Exhibit patience, which is defined as a quiet, uncomplaining endurance of stressful and annoying situations. Some people can be annoying; however, I have found that most people willing to submit to a Bible study are good listeners and are truly hungry for God's Word.

Invite Your Students to Church

Again, at the right time, invite your students to church—but don't pressure them. And when your students come to church, introduce them to many people. Form a support group for them. Sit with them if necessary. Make them feel at home in the body of Christ. Introduce them to others so that they become comfortable with the church—and so that you can start looking for someone else to disciple!

Teaching a Bible study and watching a sinner's face light up with hope is exciting. There is no greater thrill than to witness the change in a person's heart. Of course, not all of our students will give their lives to Christ. But that is not our responsibility. We are responsible to sow the seed. It is not our fault when, after we have taught the Word, our student makes the decision not to serve the Lord. We may feel discouraged because we have expended much time and energy with the individual in hopes of winning them to Christ. God understands this, and He will reward us for our effort—not for the results of our effort. We may never know it, but the seed that we have planted may lie dormant for a time and suddenly, years down the road, begin to grow. Sow the seed, pray for them, be a friend, and then leave them to God.

Give home Bible studies a try. You will be surprised what you are capable of doing with God's anointing. Of course, we won't all teach with the same personality or use the same techniques, but if we will allow the Lord to speak through us, all of us can sow the seed of the gospel. And remember that it is not so much which Bible study you teach, but rather, that by meeting with your sinner friend week after week, you are developing a relationship with this person in order to lead him or her to Christ.

If you are feeling the burden to win someone to

Christ right now, why don't you take just a moment to pray and ask God to give you strength to overcome your fear and other insecurities so that you can do a work for the Lord. You might pray something like this:

"Lord Jesus, I desire to win sinners to You. Help me to look through Your eyes and see the destitute state of Your children. Take my insecurities and strengthen me through Your Word and Holy Spirit. Take my fear and replace it with spiritual boldness. Grant me wisdom so that I can be used by You to meet the sinner's needs. I realize that I am living in the closing days of time, so help me to rearrange my busy schedule so that I may fulfill Your will in my life. I give You all the praise and glory for every soul that will be won to Your kingdom. In Jesus' name I pray. Amen."

If you are reading this book, it is because you are interested in soulwinning. Perhaps you have felt restless, discontented, or even unhappy. You may feel that since you are a child of God, you should not be having these feelings. It could be that God is speaking to your heart and wanting you to serve others by sowing the gospel seed. Remember that I taught in an earlier chapter that even people who do not know God understand that happiness comes with serving others and that Jesus prescribed serving others as a way of life. Jesus said, "If ye know these things, happy are ye if ye do them" (John 13:17). Soulwinning is an act of service to both God and mankind. God's Spirit within is urging us to fulfill the great commission.

Summary of Guidelines for Successful Home Bible Studies

- Always protect your and your students' reputations.
- The week before your first lesson, pray and fast.
- Always begin and end a Bible study with prayer.
- Ask your students to hold most questions until the end of the lesson.
- Make sure that you and your students are comfortable.
- Never read the lesson or memorize it word for word.
- Don't read too many verses of Scripture.
- Don't give too much information.
- Give handouts to your students.
- Make your lessons interesting.
- Carefully illustrate that every lesson has a spiritual application and is relevant to our lives.
- Stress your students' need of salvation.
- Know what is happening in world news.
- Reschedule a canceled lesson as soon as possible.
- Love and befriend your students.
- Refuse to argue.
- Never get angry.
- Invite your students to church.

Part Three

SERVING

"My little children, of whom I travail in birth again until Christ be formed in you" (Galatians 4:19).

A mother is awakened in the middle of the night by an insistent small voice within, "Mommy, I'm ready to be born." In just a few minutes, a second contraction takes her breath away. The hours ahead will take every ounce of her strength and even bring her to the threshold of death, and yet she eagerly looks forward to the reward at the end of her labor. When the doctor announces the birth of the baby boy or girl, great awe fills the room. In ecstatic joy, the new parents are elevated beyond this world. All thought of the hard labor is dismissed. The parents, nurses, and physicians look on in wonder. Although countless billions have been born into this world, birth never loses its wonder. It is as if with the wail of a newborn, the Spirit of God breathes new hope into the world. New life is worth travail.

CHAPTER SIX

Travail Begins at Birth

"A woman when she is in travail hath sorrow, because her hour is come: but as soon as she is delivered of the child, she remembereth no more the anguish, for joy that a man is born into the world" (John 16:21). Childbirth is hard work—that's why it is called labor. Labor, however, is not without its reward, for with the newborn's first wail, joy is born. The mother quickly forgets the agony of childbirth. Fathers glow with pride as if they have just won the Nobel Prize. Grandparents show off pictures and wear "Ask Me About My Grandchild" pins. Aunties and uncles, cousins, brothers and sisters all join in the excitement at the birth of a baby. The family unit is forever changed.

After the initial burst of excitement dies down a bit, and the parents have experienced the first night home with their little bundle of joy, reality begins to set in. The birthing pains may be in the past, but the long arduous work of raising the child has just begun. A great deal of nurturing and training must take place before that child will reach maturity and take his or her place in society.

Spiritual childbirth is much like natural childbirth in that they both require a great amount of labor and both have joy as their reward. They also share a similar responsibility to the newborn. Just as we cannot neglect a growing child, Christ would not have us neglect a newborn soul. We must labor to bring newborn souls to maturity in Christ.

Recently in the news from the Saint Louis area, a mother gave birth to twin baby girls. When it became financially difficult to care for the girls, she auctioned them off to the highest bidder! Sadly, this and similar scenarios take place over and over again. Some parents are worse than infidels when they abandon their newborns in bathrooms or dumpsters. We are outraged when people bring children into the world and then decide that they do not want the responsibility of raising them. Should we feel any different when newborns are born into the church and then, through neglect, are permitted to slip back into sin? We pray for God to send us babies, and when they come, do we take responsibility to lead them to maturity in Christ?

Bringing children, spiritual or natural, into the world implies a life of service. Parents train up their children in the natural sense so that, when the children are grown, they will make a contribution to society. So we too must train up newborn Christians to maturity so that they will make a contribution to the kingdom of God.

The years I spent raising my children to love the Lord and the church and preparing myself by studying His Word was what I like to think of as my wilderness training for a future of raising spiritual newborns. The wilderness is a time of preparation. We read about Moses who spent forty years in the wilderness preparing to lead the Israelites out of captivity. Paul spent three years in the wilderness with Jesus preparing to take the gospel to the Gentiles. Jesus spent forty days and forty nights in the wilderness before beginning His ministry. The wilderness I went through prepared me for what God wanted to do with me.

It was a privilege to teach my children the ways of God. It is also a privilege to work with God to help newborn saints grow to maturity. To illustrate the importance of discipleship and how I have discipled a new believer, I will share aspects of my relationship with a young woman named Melanie. She tested my mothering skills to the max. I learned from her that a newborn saint, just like my children, has many needs—spiritual as well as physical. With my children as well as with Melanie, I learned to love God's way: unconditionally. I learned how to listen. I learned patience. I learned how to travail.

Melanie's situation seemed impossible, but through

obedience to His will, the impossible became possible. Her complete transformation emphasizes the value of a soul. It is my hope that Melanie's conversion and journey toward maturity will inspire others to parent someone to Christ.

CHAPTER SEVEN

Melanie's Conversion

In the prayer room, I have often prayed and heard others praying, "Convict the sinners of our city and compel them by Your Spirit to come into the house of God where they will hear the message of salvation." God hears us when we pray. Melanie, no doubt, is one of those answered prayers. Melanie's conversion is a classic example of God's mercy and grace. Melanie's transformation began when the Spirit of God spoke to her heart and she found herself in an apostolic church service. When the altar call was given, she obeyed and walked to the altar. I found myself beside her as she wept and cried out to God. I saw her anguish and tears. I heard her repent. I prayed with her and saw her nod her head when asked if she would like to be baptized. From somewhere behind me, I heard the pastor say, "This one is going to need a lot of help." Those prophetic words fell on my heart. I didn't know it then, but the burden to help Melanie would weigh heavily upon me until I obeyed. Years later, I asked the pastor if he remembered saying those words. He did not. I shall always believe God spoke to me through him.

It is expected of pastors as servants of Christ to labor for souls, but do we do our part to assist him or her? My guess is that as saints in the church, we need to do more to help carry the burden for lost souls. In the fall of 1995, at a ladies' conference in Cincinnati, Ohio, Sister Nona Freeman, missionary to Africa, said, "It is not the shepherd who gives birth to the little lambs; the sheep do." She referred to the shepherd as our pastor, and we, or the saints, as the sheep. Shepherds carefully watch over their flock. They protect them from danger and lead them to greener pastures. Jesus commanded Peter to feed his sheep (John 21:16-17). Our shepherd-pastors feed and protect us from the dangers of this life. Their job is enormous. While good pastors will labor for the sheep, we should not expect them to do all the work. They need our help! We can help carry the burden by doing our part in nurturing and grounding newborn saints in the truth.

After mentoring Melanie, I fully understand the pastor's need for the sheep to give birth to the little lambs. If we consider the devastated condition that people are in when they are born into our churches, we will realize that our pastors simply do not have enough hours in the day to give full attention to the needs of these newborn saints. The baggage that people bring with them when they come to Christ is so heavy that it takes a strong saint to help them toss it all away. They come steeped in such awful sins that, to our natural eyes, we would say there is no hope. Some like my friend Melanie require months and even years of help. Pastors cannot possibly bring every newborn to maturity. When we travail with new converts, our pastor has more time to see to the general well-being of the church.

At the time God brought Melanie into my life, I was working part-time in an office, and I was very unhappy. Life surely was more than shuffling papers! The more I thought of the futility of life, the unhappier I became. My restless soul was feeling the urging of the Holy Spirit within to do what He had called me to do. I had a habit of talking to God while I worked, and God began to talk to me. At the forefront of my mind, I could hear the Lord say, "Visit Melanie after you leave the office." I came up with every excuse possible. "But God, I don't know her." She had only been to church a few times. "What if she is a nut?" (I later found out that she indeed was a nut—a good kind of nut!) "What if I don't like her?" Not like Melanie, impossible. She is like a puppy; no one can resist a puppy. She makes you feel good just being around her. Like Moses I pulled the old "I won't know what to say to her or how to witness to her" excuse. All the way home, I argued with God. As I was nearing her house, the urgency to stop rose up within me. I gripped the steering wheel and argued out loud, "You don't understand, God. I just can't; I just can't!" As I started to pass her house, at the last possible moment, I hit the brakes, whipped the steering wheel to the left, and drove up her bumpy, gravel driveway.

"Okay, Lord, I'm here. You have to help me." I looked at her tiny, country blue house. It wasn't any bigger than a very small cottage you might see near a lake. I got out of the car and determinedly walked up to the door. I felt the Holy Spirit strengthen me. I knocked. I saw a curtain move. I knocked again. I thought, "She sees me. She doesn't want to talk to me!" "*Keep knocking*," a voice from within cried. Finally, she answered the door and reluctantly invited me in. We started with light chitchat. "How is your day going. What about this weather?" Like at that moment either of us really cared about the weather! We were busy sizing up one another. Suddenly to my complete surprise, she blurted out, "I don't want anything to do with your church. I heard that you can't wear pants, and I like my jeans!" With a sinking feeling, I thought to myself, *Who told you that you can't wear pants?* A well-meaning saint had spilled the proverbial holiness-standard beans. She must have missed the lesson where the pastor told us that you can't filet the fish before catching it! I immediately began back-paddling to right this indiscretion. I was beginning to sweat, but to my surprise, instead of backing down I boldly replied, "You need to understand some things about the Word of God, and I think a Bible study would help you." (The power of the Spirit was working within!) Just as boldly she challenged, "You show me in the Bible where I can't wear my jeans. And while you are at it, show me where it says I can't cut my hair or wear jewelry. My mother just bought me this gold cross for my birthday, and I am not ever taking it off my neck." Taking a deep breath and uttering a silent prayer of *Oh, help me, Lord Jesus,* I sat down on her couch and opened my Bible. You talk about dueling banjos. We were just beginning what was to be many years of a one-on-one relationship.

The Holy Spirit within me went straight to work on me as well as Melanie when I opened my Bible to the following scriptures concerning the issues that she had mentioned: hair, clothing, and jewelry.

> "But if a woman have long hair, it is a glory to her: for *her* hair is given her for a covering" (I Corinthians 11:15).

> "The woman shall not wear that which pertaineth unto a man, neither shall a man put on a woman's garment: for all that do so *are* abomination unto the LORD thy God" (Deuteronomy 22:5).

> "Whose adorning let it not be that outward *adorning* of plaiting the hair, and of wearing of gold, or of putting on of apparel" (I Peter 3:3).

Needless to say, a simple Bible study ensued with the Spirit within doing most of the teaching. I was not very adept in those days at wielding the sword of truth. In fact, it was my relationship to Melanie that drove me to seek a Christian education degree. Of course, anyone can learn to rightly divide the Word without a degree. On that first day with Melanie, I read these scriptures and allowed God to reveal truth to Melanie's heart, with very little of my own input on the subjects. I had always obeyed the scriptures concerning holiness but was never certain how to explain them to others. The desire to see Melanie saved caused me to improve my prayer life and knowledge of the Word. To make a long story short, Melanie eventually took off her gold cross, gave away her jeans, and let her hair grow. To God be the glory!

Unfortunately, statistics say that a vast majority of people we witness to never come to the Lord. But when they do, and when we take the time to disciple them, we experience great joy and fulfillment in our lives. Every time I talk with Melanie, without fail she mentions how grateful she is that God put me in her life. I am just as quick to tell her that it is I who am grateful to her. Because of her many needs, I had to grow up in the Lord. I have learned a great truth in my work with Melanie: while the soulwinner is a blessing to the sinner, the new convert becomes an even greater blessing to the soulwinner. Soulwinning is a win-win situation no matter the outcome. We can never lose when we are doing the will of God.

As I look back over the months before meeting Melanie, I realize that the Lord was preparing me for what I was about to go through with her. A month or two before I met her, I felt compelled in my spirit to study I Corinthians 13. I read and re-read that chapter for a month or more. At the time, I didn't know why I was studying the "love chapter," but I remember trying so hard to hide that precious advice in my heart. Not until Melanie came into my life would I realize why the Spirit impressed me to study this chapter on love. It would take a genuine, godly love to help Melanie's tormented, battered soul. She needed a friend who would give her unconditional love. God had chosen me to be that friend.

Love grew as I sat in her living room on that first visit to Melanie's home. I listened to what was to become literally hours of days of listening. Could she ever talk and did she ever have problems! Surely no one in the entire world had as many difficulties as my new friend. Having never been out in the world much, and definitely having never experienced the horrendous sins that Melanie had been involved in, I was deeply disturbed and moved with compassion for her. So listening for hours on end was my destiny. I could not have done it without the love of Christ's Spirit to strengthen me.

Melanie's walk with Jesus began on a sunny, October day in which she intended to end her life. God, however, had different plans for this young lady. She wasn't getting out of this world that easy! She had a child to raise and a job to fulfill in the kingdom of God. She would begin an odyssey that would lead her from the brink of hell to a victorious life in Christ. Miraculously, the same night that she intended to end her life, she was baptized in Jesus' name! In the weeks ahead, God would work through me to mentor her.

Prior to her baptism, Melanie was a very unhappy young woman who drowned her problems in alcohol. One day about three weeks before coming to the Lord, she got fed up with her drinking lifestyle and quit. She told me that God took away her drinking habit so that He could speak to her heart. Although she sometimes felt the prodding of God on her heart, she could never fully hear His voice when she was drunk. Drowning her sorrows, alcohol also dulled her senses. Without the alcohol, life looked hopeless. One morning, she woke severely depressed. She felt like she had nothing to live for. She felt that her mother, father, sister, and brother did not love her. She did not even believe her husband loved her. She lit cigarette after cigarette. Emotionally, she was a mess. She had one thing that she loved with all her heart: her little boy. In such a miserable state of despair, even he was not enough to prevent her from wanting to take her life. Her heart was aching and crying,

"Is there anyone who loves me?" You and I did not hear her cry, but thank God there is a loving Savior who hears when His babies sincerely cry out. He would give her a reason to live.

On October 14, 1990, God began to speak ever so gently to her bruised heart. She remembered a little church that she had gone to years before as a child. Something urged her to go to the church. She was looking for a reason to live and someone to love her. In her car, she sped past an apostolic church next door to her house. Urgently, God spoke to her heart. She turned into a parking lot just past the church and drove back to it. She found the church door locked and began knocking. When no one responded, she walked around to the chapel door. Normally all the doors of the church are kept locked, but this particular Sunday afternoon, she found that the chapel door was held open with a tiny rock. To this day, she insists that Jesus, her Rock, had left that door open for her! And I just happen to believe that God did indeed allow that stone to be in the door for Melanie.

A wedding had been at the church the day before, and the bride's father was cleaning up. This brother in the Lord delighted in witnessing. Surely it was not an accident that the Lord brought these two together that gloriously fateful day. Later, this man's wife was to become one of Melanie's dearest friends and confidantes. I was not to be the only one who would be used to mentor this dear child of God. The man at the church spoke to her about the Lord and invited her to Sunday evening service. Melanie came to church and was baptized that night. The Lord washed all of her sins away and gave her hope, but it would be literally years before Melanie would completely yield her will to the Savior.

A few weeks after my first visit to Melanie's home and her consent to a Bible study, my husband and I began a home Bible study with her and her husband. Her husband was baptized a few weeks later. We both immediately took a liking to him. It is important to note that this couple had just moved back to Ohio, where Melanie's family lived. Having been in Ohio only a short time, they had few friends and were understandably lonely. Now that they both had been baptized, they needed Christian friends. As I have already mentioned, support groups for new converts are a very important need within the church. New converts should be introduced to as many people as soon as possible. If introduced to many different people, friendships will develop.

Let me emphasize once again how important it is to make all visitors to our churches feel welcome. I have had personal experience in facing a sea of strangers when visiting other churches. I consider myself a well-adjusted saint, and yet, when I visit other churches, I become overwhelmed with shyness. I feel like a duck in the wrong pond! Visitors can quickly be put at ease when one or more individuals take it upon themselves to speak to them or even invite them to sit with them during the service.

Since we were teaching a husband and wife, my husband, Bob, decided to teach the Bible study, at least for the first few weeks. We chose to begin the study in the New Testament because both had already been baptized, and we felt an urgency to explain what they had experienced. Today, if we found ourselves in this situation, we would use one of the smaller studies first, such as *Into His Marvelous Light,* to provide immediate understanding of salvation. Most often, it is preferable to begin in the Old Testament so that a full understanding of God's plan for man from the beginning of creation is revealed. Another reason we began in the New Testament was because they needed to understand the baptism of the Holy Spirit and hopefully receive it as soon as possible.

As my husband began the study, both husband and wife listened intently and asked questions. They were considerate to hold most questions to the end of the session so that we could finish the study within the recommended sixty minutes. At the end of each session, we spent just a few minutes with light chitchat and then left so as not to wear out our welcome.

Melanie studied the Word diligently. Every day she would search the Scriptures for herself and quickly learned how to cross-reference. Cross-referencing often led her into areas where the Lord spoke specifically to her. Often she would call me to ask a question about a certain scripture that she did not quite understand.

Melanie quickly fell in love with God's Word. She also learned to pray. She devoted time to Bible reading and prayer every day. She learned that prayer was her lifeline. I don't know anyone who struggled with the flesh any more than Melanie did, but neither do I know anyone who so completely trusted God to help conquer the flesh like Melanie did. Her faith and obedience to God are what have brought her through her first eleven years in kingdom living. She specifically asked me to tell you that, if it wasn't for God's patient love and mercy over and over again, she would not be where she is today. Melanie has no doubt that she owes her life to Jesus.

When we look at people, we can only see the outward condition, and we often think that it is impossible for God to save that individual. But God looks on the heart. He sees the possibility in us and not the impossibility. Who would have guessed a young woman like Melanie would ever become one of God's dearest children? Often I teasingly say to God, "You know You love her better than You do me." I am so glad that our Savior is not a respecter of persons.

I can't express enough just how important it is to become involved in the life of the person you hope to disciple. Early in our relationship, Melanie and I spent much time together. One day, while walking through some fields between our homes, we found an old, wild cherry tree. Melanie and I laughed and had a wonderful time as we picked and pitted those cherries. I taught her to make a cherry pie, which she proudly presented to her husband that evening. I didn't know how to disciple a new baby in Christ, but I lent myself to God's will, and He taught me one day at a time, just as his Word says: "For precept *must* be upon precept . . . line upon line . . . here a little, *and* there a little" (Isaiah 28:10).

Travailing until an individual reaches maturity does not mean that we have to spend every waking moment with him or her, but we will have to invest a certain amount of time. Our goal is to be like Paul and travail until Christ is formed within the newborn, and that means learning to do whatever it takes to bring the baby to maturity. We will have to become patient listeners, who are "swift to hear, slow to speak" (James 1:19).

Again, developing relationships is the name of the game. It is the bottom line. If we really want to see a soul grounded in the church, we must follow through. This is what it means to travail. We may plan visits with our new spiritual babies, call them on the phone to tell them we are thinking about them, bake them dinner or dessert, or send a note of encouragement from time to time.

Men are different from women. They could, of course, make a phone call, plan a lunch engagement, schedule a game of golf, or invite their new baby to watch or play softball or basketball. Methods of travail are limited only to our own creativity and sensitivity to individual needs. When our newborns come to church, we must always watch for them and speak to them. Again, if they come to church by themselves, we should sit with them. It is of utmost importance that we do not allow them to feel alone. Introduce them to many different people. The church is a family, and a family provides a loving, safe place for its members.

The night Melanie received the Holy Spirit was a special "singspiration" service. Melanie came in by herself that night, and the Holy Spirit prompted me to sit with her—something I had never done before. I fought it for a little bit; after all, I had my seat on the far right, and she was seated on the far left. I was not really anxious to move. After several minutes of prodding, I heeded the voice of the Lord and moved. We sat together and toward the end of the service, when asked to stand for the closing song, I felt the Holy Spirit prompt me again, and I told Melanie that this was her night to receive the Holy Spirit. She worshiped the Lord with all her heart, and God filled her with the Holy Spirit right there in our pew. She was so excited! As we walked out the back doors after church, she turned to me and said, "Does this mean that I am going to go to heaven now?" When I said yes, that girl screamed so shrilly that I thought my eardrums would break, and every head in the parking lot turned to see who was being killed. She was one happy newborn. I was overwhelmed. I had helped a sinner find Jesus. *What joy*! My work was done. I could rest and go on to another sinner. Wrong! My job was just beginning. I was about to learn the true meaning of travail.

CHAPTER EIGHT

Watching for Her Soul

The first Sunday morning that Melanie missed coming to church, I called her on the telephone. I really didn't want to do it, but the Holy Spirit would not let me alone. A few years before I knew Melanie, my aunt had returned to church from a backslidden state. My husband and I picked her up for church, but one particular Sunday she called and told us not to come for her. Instead of me asking why, I just let her go. What a dreadful mistake. She backslid the second time for many years. Her children were grown before she got back into church. Oh, how I have repented for my failure of not trying to prevent this from happening! So when I noticed that Melanie was not in church on Sunday morning, I obeyed the prompting of the Spirit and called her. I learned that she had decided to go boating that morning with her father. After all, she explained, "It was a perfect morning to be out on the lake." Many times she has thanked me for explaining to her that you have to be faithful to the house of God. Yes, she was angry with me that day for having the audacity to tell her that she had to be in church, but she was there that Sunday night and every service since! In fact, she is still not convinced that it is okay to stay home when you are sick or in the hospital. She is the epitome of faithfulness.

In the early years with Melanie, at least once a day, the phone would ring and I would hear an irrational, screaming voice—usually full of frustration. Most of the time she never bothered to say hello or give her name, she just plunged into whatever was troubling her, from a spiritual failure to faulty attempts to win her family to God. Sometimes she just called to give me a victory report. Sometimes the phone would ring and nobody would be on the line. Later, she confessed to me that she thought the Rapture had taken place and wanted to make sure that I was still at home. She figured if I answered, she was safe.

Oh, how I have learned to love this dear woman. Life with her is never dull. There were times when she wore me to a frazzle with her frustrations. She believes that I have all the answers, and I do: She like every one of us needs Jesus. I am not a professional counselor, but I know the only true Counselor: Jesus Christ. I trust that His Word can handle any difficulty. In learning to travail with Melanie, I confess that I found myself in the pastor's office many times to receive counseling and encouragement for myself.

Weeks of listening to this young lady soon made me aware that there were probably very few, if any sins that had not touched her life. You name it; she had done it or had been the victim of it. Her baggage was so heavy that God knew she needed someone to help her unload it. Why He chose me with all my inexperience, I will never understand. She needed so much more than I felt I was capable of giving her. I don't take credit for her salvation, because all I did was lend myself to the Lord and allowed Him to work through me.

After her conversion, by the grace of God, Melanie gave up one sin after another. She quickly learned to speak without cursing. It took Melanie a couple of years to totally give up cigarettes and other vices, but she did get the victory over them! The greatest joy a soulwinner will ever experience has been mine as I have watched Melanie grow in the Lord. I am thankful that God chose me to help disciple her and to help her grow to maturity in Christ. My experience with Melanie has taught me many things, but one lesson stands out from all the others: We must be very careful to give our partner in soulwinning, the Holy Spirit, all the glory. I greatly admire Melanie's tenacity to hold to God despite all obstacles. I feel that if someone with the sin-load that Melanie came to church with can live for God, anyone with a desire to serve God can do it. She still carries many scars from her past and fights many battles with the flesh, but she is definitely an overcomer. A winner never quits, and a quitter never wins. Melanie is a winner, and I am rooting her on all the way to the finish line.

In conclusion, the time for revival is ripe, not only in America, but throughout our world. While it is a day of uncertainty for many, it is an exciting day for the child of God. The Holy Spirit is urging us to work while it is yet day, for darkness is coming quickly upon us. We are on a mission with God's power within us. You can be a soulwinner. You can lead others to maturity in Christ. Make yourself available to God and let His Holy Spirit empower you to do a mighty work for Him.

About the Author

Dawn and her husband, Robert, attend the Apostolic Church of Barberton, Ohio, pastored by Rodney V. Pamer. They have three married sons and are grandparents. Over the past twenty-six years, she has been involved in many aspects of the church, which include teaching Sunday school and adult Bible study classes, greeting visitors, and working with young people. She received a bachelor's of Religious Education from Apostolic Bible College in Memphis, Tennessee in 1998. During a brief stay in Missouri, she was a volunteer for World Network of Prayer. One of her special interests is writing. Over the years, she has written many short articles for her local assembly and two national publications of the Assemblies of the Lord Jesus Christ—*Today's Apostolic Woman* and *The Apostolic Witness.*

Search for Truth #1

A 10-lesson Bible study course with two-color charts that covers the entire Bible. Charts available in two sizes.

Certificates (25)		
70-1-88096-913-3	Paper	**$8.95**
Large Chart (19" x 25")		
70-1-88096-912-3	English	**$34.95**
70-1-88096-913-9	Español	**$34.95**
Mini Carrying Case (9" x 11")		
Will hold mini chart and teacher's manual.		
70-0-7577-0649-5	Vinyl	**$12.99**
Mini Chart (8-1/2" x 11")		
70-1-88096-912-6	English	**$13.95**
70-1-88096-913-4	Español	**$13.95**
Student Study Sheets (10)		
70-1-88096-912-7	English	**$9.95**
70-1-88096-913-8	Español	**$9.95**
Teacher's Manual		
70-1-88096-912-4	English	**$12.95**
70-1-88096-913-5	Español	**$12.95**

Search for Truth #2

A 12-lesson introduction to the Bible. Charts in beautiful four-color and available in two sizes.

Carrying Case (11" x 14")		
Will hold 3-ring binder, mini chart, and teacher's manual.		
70-0-7577-0660-6	Vinyl	**$18.99**
CD-ROM		
70-0-7577-2373-X	Software	**$19.99**
Large Carrying Case (31" x 3" x 23")		
70-0-7577-1042-5	Vinyl	**$31.99**
Large Chart (19" x 25")		
70-1-88096-913-2	Spiral-bound	**$64.95**
Mini Chart (8-1.2" x 11")		
70-1-88096-913-7	Spiral-bound	**$25.95**
Student Study Sheets (10)		
70-1-88096-913-6	Paper	**$12.95**
Teacher's Manual		
70-1-88096-913-1	Paper	**$21.95**
Transparencies (82)		
70-0-7577-0671-1		**$179.95**

order form

Product Name	Item #	Qty	Price	Total

Customer ID #: ______________________________

Name ______________________________

Address ______________________________

City ____________________ St.____ Zip __________

Phone ______________ E-Mail ______________

Charge my: _____Disc _____M/C _____Visa _____Amex

Credit Card No. ______________________________

Exp. Date Mo. ______ Yr. ______ ____________________

Signature as it appears on credit card

If items not in stock backorder ___Yes ___No

To Order Contact:

Pentecostal Publishing House, 8855 Dunn Rd., Hazelwood, MO 63042-2299

Call: 314-336-1818

Fax: 314-837-6574

E-mail: pphsales@upci.org

Or Visit: www.pentecostalpublishing.com